Refining Common Sense

Moving from Data to Information

Vickie Williams Phelps
Elizabeth F. Warren

SCARECROWEDUCATION
Lanham, Maryland • Toronto • Oxford
2004

Published in the United States of America
by ScarecrowEducation
An imprint of The Rowman & Littlefield Publishing Group, Inc.
4501 Forbes Boulevard, Suite 200, Lanham, Maryland 20706
www.scarecroweducation.com

PO Box 317
Oxford
OX2 9RU, UK

Illustrations by Suzanne L. Huser

British Library Cataloguing in Publication Information Available

Library of Congress Cataloging-in-Publication Data

Phelps, Vickie Williams, 1949–
    Refining common sense : moving from data to information / Vickie
    Williams Phelps, Elizabeth F. Warren.
    p. cm.
    Includes bibliographical references and index.
    ISBN 1-57886-046-6 (pbk. : alk. paper)
    1. Educational statistics. 2. School management and organization. I.
    Warren, Elizabeth F., 1951– II. Title.
    LB2846 .P47 2004
    370'.2'1—dc22
                                                          2003019662

♾™ The paper used in this publication meets the minimum requirements of
American National Standard for Information Sciences—Permanence of Paper
for Printed Library Materials, ANSI/NISO Z39.48-1992.
Manufactured in the United States of America.

Contents

Foreword

TetraData Corporation is an education software and services company that focuses on data warehousing, analysis, assessment, and improvement in education. TetraData is proudly associated with Drs. Vickie W. Phelps and Elizabeth F. Warren, two of the most dedicated, capable and knowledgeable education leaders that we have met in our education technology journey. Our firm shares a common passion, i.e., that information-driven decision-making can provide each district, each school, and each class with a reliable way to facilitate improved learning. We also share a common commitment to make information-driven decision making a practical and working part of the challenging and busy education process.

Vickie and Liz's book *Refining Common Sense* fills a much-needed gap in the industry. This book is a great tool—a handbook as the authors describe it—that deals with the practical planning, processes, and even forms that are needed to prepare and implement information-driven decision-making. With years of hands-on education system experience under their belts and with a passion for every position in the organization, i.e., teachers, principals, program directors, superintendents, board members, parents, students, and support staff, they bring their own successes and experiences to life in what they deliver in this publication. They have been living information-driven decision-making for longer than I have known them, i.e., more than 5½ years. They are both practitioners at heart and bring the content right to the person who is working day to day to make tough decisions with limited resources.

v

What I enjoyed immensely about this publication is that Drs. Phelps and Warren have taken the technology aspects of information-driven decision-making and presented the information in a clear and understandable fashion. Whether the topic is data warehousing or data cleansing, they have made the issues lucid and approachable. This is extremely important since one of the major barriers to educators being able to deal with data-analysis systems is the challenge in sorting out the role and value proposition of technology. These two educators have listened to educators, to technologists and placed the software in its proper place, i.e., tools that can assist the process, rather than the answer to the difficult questions. They rightly encourage and guide readers to the processes that enable people to make information-driven decision-making work successfully.

One of the major education issues that this book handles is the question "What do I do when I first implement a data-analysis system?" This is key. We have seen numerous districts and schools struggle with that first step: "What are the first reports that I should analyze; what queries start this process?" This book does not hold back the rich experience that these ladies have lived. It goes right at the need and provides you with the rich content to help you start your information-driven decision-making journey, as well as keep it going. This handbook touches the needs of numerous individuals in the education network, from the teacher who needs to understand the capabilities of her individual students to school principals, counselors, instructional coordinators, testing and analysis coordinators, program directors, grant writers, district researchers, and certainly the district executives. By virtue of their rich education experience, Drs. Phelps and Warren have given everyone in education, including the nontechnologists, an opportunity to benefit from this fine publication. I encourage your reading of this book and the further encouraging of your school, your district, to benefit from the extensive experience these two practitioners have provided for all our benefit. Enjoy this wonderful handbook and let it drive all of us to focus on our future, our children.

Martin S. Brutosky
Chairman and CEO, TetraData Corporation

Acknowledgments

We would like to thank TetraData Corporation for allowing us to use demonstration databases in their EASE-e Data Analysis Suite for many of our school district data examples. Our thanks also goes to Suzanne Huser for her original artwork.

Introduction

What makes Deming attractive is that his work represents a refinement of common sense. (Schmoker and Wilson 1993, 8)

When we look back at the improvements made in education in the United States during the last few decades, we see that, in many ways, W. Edwards Deming started them all. His focus on systems thinking has become the underpinning for much of today's very best practices in schools.

We call this book *Refining Common Sense* because of a statement that caught our attention in Schmoker and Wilson's 1993 book, *Total Quality Education*, "Improvement is possible and essential. The development of human beings by using the talent they bring to their work cannot help but result in improvement . . . on the whole, what makes Deming attractive is that his work represents a refinement of common sense" (p. 8).

One of the key components of Deming's systems thinking is the use of data to make decisions. We had been reading about, thinking about, and working with data to make decisions even before we read Schmoker's 1996 book titled *Results*. After we read his book, we became even more conscious of the value that information-driven decisions bring to our organizations.

We've continued to find and read information about data-driven decision-making in a variety of places—a number of excellent books and articles have been written on the subject. Many books also have a good chapter or two about data-driven decision-making within a broader context.

But during the last year or two, we've become frustrated, because, while many people are writing about using data to make decisions and many are writing primers on statistics for educators, we think that a key component is missing. We haven't seen anything that gives educators the tools to develop a clear, easy-to-follow road map. As we began our data journey, we needed a road map to lead us from the big policy decisions about the kinds of questions to ask, to decisions about the kinds of data to collect and how to collect it, and all the way down the road to using the information we generated in our decision-making. We took many unnecessary detours along the way. This handbook is designed to help you develop your own road map to lead you more directly to your information-driven decision-making goals.

You would not be reading this book if you were not working to improve student learning. But even as we all work toward the same goal, we are all starting from different places. We take very different routes to our ultimate destination. For that reason, we can't give you *the one* road map. There simply isn't a single route that will do for all educators in all schools working with all students. There isn't one road map, because, as we all know, there isn't one road. Use this handbook to develop your own road map for your journey. Use it to help you systematically make decisions based on the information you gain from analyzing data.

How is this handbook different from other books you'll read on data-driven decision-making?

First, this handbook is a tool, not just a book. It is designed to be your companion and guide as you work, step by step, through the process of asking questions, collecting data, and determining the answers to your questions based on your information.

Second, this handbook comes with a compact disk with templates for forms you can fill in as you work through the process. If you would rather use a hard copy, you can print each form to complete as you go through the process.

Third, this handbook includes a testing and measurements primer to refer to as you analyze test data.

Finally, although we often use the term data-driven because that occurs most frequently in the literature, what we really want to show you is how to make "information-driven" decisions. Information-driven decisions come about as a result of asking the right questions, collecting the right data, appropriately analyzing the data, and reporting the data in ways that clearly reveal the issues and answers surrounding student achievement. Data give us information. Information gives us the foundation upon which to make better decisions.

> **As a general rule the most successful man in life is the man who has the best information. (Benjamin Disraeli, 1804–1881)**

Information becomes the foundation for knowledge, which in turn is the basis for wise decisions. When we talk about making data-driven decisions, we are talking about one of the elemental steps in the process. Transforming data to information makes wise decisions possible.

As you follow this step-by-step guide, you will have a clear road map for making information-based decisions. When you have your road map, we will have met our goal in designing this handbook for you to use.

PREMISES

This handbook is based on the following premises:

- We know that schools must continually improve for our students to learn more.
- We know that information-driven decision-making is a critical component of school improvement.
- We know that analyzing data is necessary, but not in and of itself sufficient for school improvement.
- We know that many people are not comfortable using data.
- We know that what passes for research is many times really just data-gathering.
- We know that tools are available to help us manipulate data easily.
- We know that data must be turned into information to be used.
- We know that many people misunderstand and misuse data and testing information.

Establishing relationships among data and making decisions based on data can be tricky. A basic knowledge of tests and measurements and a healthy dose of common sense are required. This book will help you plot a path toward a better sense of those relationships, a more thorough understanding of tests and measures, and a little more focus for your own common sense about the use of data.

Part 1

GETTING STARTED WITH DATA

You're starting down the information-based decision-making road. We promise you won't forget the trip. There are a few things you need to gather before you leave.

First, since the trip could be a long one, imagine that you will be taking the trip in the vehicle of your dreams—that convertible, SUV, luxury sedan, pickup truck, or chartered bus. Second, think about who is going with you. You'll need some good navigators and some help with the driving. Third, you might want to take a snack box and a cooler—you're going to need to keep your strength up. Finally, you need to have a destination in mind, one that you've determined through a goal-setting process. Now, you're all set.

Well, not exactly. Do you know how you're going to get there?

This trip is through the world of turning your data into information to make decisions. Part 1 will help you take the data you have and transform them into information.

1

Thinking about Data

Using data separates good schools from mediocre schools.
(Killion and Bellamy 2000, 1)

WHY ANALYZE DATA?

Data analysis has one purpose—to turn data into information so that you can use that information to make decisions.

Anyone who needs to make good decisions needs to analyze data. According to W. Edwards Deming, "Management in any form is prediction" (Schmoker and Wilson 1993, 21). You can say the same about leadership. Leaders in school systems—leaders at all levels—need to be able to make predictions. Data analysis is one of the best tools available to help you accomplish that task.

The purpose of having data-based information is to help you determine what is working in your system and what is not working so that you can keep—and build on—what is working while you change what is not working. Leaders must be absolutely committed to purposeful action that supports successful practices while changing practices that institutionalize failure. To do those two things, leaders need information. To get information that is valuable, leaders start by asking questions.

The questions you decide to answer should depend directly on your system's goals. So begin by looking at your goals. Your goals provide the

context within which you ask your questions. You are going to gather data to answer the questions that tell you whether you are reaching your goals. The process is as simple—and as profound—as that.

WHAT DECISIONS SHOULD INVOLVE DATA ANALYSIS?

All of them. Or at least all the ones that people within a school system make that have an impact on student learning—and that should be all of them.

Sometimes the answer you need to make your decision will leap off the page of data; other times you will find it baled in large, obfuscating bundles of numbers. Sometimes you will spend only a few moments analyzing a data set; other times you will think it has become your life's work. But getting in the habit of asking, "What data do I need to analyze to help answer this question about my goal?" will serve school leaders well.

WHO SHOULD ANALYZE DATA?

In the school setting, many groups are interested in using data. Certainly parents and other members of the community want information about student progress. Our focus here is on groups that operate within the system. The five primary groups of people within a school system who need data-based information to make decisions to reach their goals are the following:

1. teachers
2. principals
3. program managers
4. superintendents
5. boards of trustees

While there is much common information that these groups of people need, each group also may need different information reported in different ways depending on the district, school, or classroom goals. We will suggest some questions that each group might consider to get you started in your thinking. Your own goals will be the real starting place.

The best way for you to use data is as a foundation for working together to identify and solve problems. Be aware that the use of data tends to threaten some people. If you don't keep that in mind, you might misinterpret their concern. While some of us look at data as emotion-free numbers to inform decisions, others find the data to be emotion-laden. The closer the numbers come to real students in your class or school, the more emotion is likely to be attached. The frame you build around the use of data can help build trust of others in both you and your use of the data. If you come in screaming, "Off with their heads!" then it's unlikely you'll find many partners in your search for data-driven decisions. Of course, that's true in all areas of decision-making and in leadership as a whole.

Mr. Olipher was in his first year as principal at Thomas Jefferson Intermediate School. He stared at the first six-week benchmark assessment scores. The scores were not good. The state was giving a new assessment this year and was providing six-week benchmark tests to help students prepare for the high-stakes test. Mr. Olipher knew that how he dealt with these first assessment scores would make a difference in how the staff regarded his leadership. It was the first time the school had given a benchmark test, so no one knew exactly what to expect. No one knew exactly what to expect from him as a new principal, either.

As he examined the scores, Mr. Olipher began to jot down the trends and patterns he saw. Three teachers' classes had overall averages significantly below the other classes' average scores in reading. Reading vocabulary scores were low across the entire fifth grade. In mathematics, scores were at the bottom of the score range across the board. Geometry scores were variable across all classes in sixth grade. Two teachers had extremely high scores in all mathematics areas. Science scores were higher in process than in content.

He put his pencil down. He thought, "I could do this analysis by myself all day. What I really need to do is think about what I'm going to do with the data with the faculty—how can we use this data as a foundation to identify problems and solve them in a way that will build trust? I think the first step is to meet with the fifth- and sixth-grade team leaders and develop a plan with them."

What suggestions would you make to Mr. Olipher and the team leaders for their plan? What pitfalls would you suggest they avoid? What situations have you experienced where data have been used to identify and solve problems in a way that built trust? What situations have you experienced where data have been used to identify and solve problems in ways that have failed to build trust?

2

Answering Questions Using Data

Successful organizations do not just collect data, they revere it. They aren't satisfied with data until data have life and meaning for every teacher, every pertinent party. They use data to create and to ensure an objective, commonly held reality. (Schmoker 2001, 51)

SHOULD YOU WORK ALONE OR WITH A TEAM?

You can develop a road map by yourself. But developing this road map is just like planning for any trip or taking a vacation. You will find that it is more powerful and more beneficial—not to mention more fun—if you develop your road map as a team. In addition, if you develop the road map alone, you may find yourself taking the journey the same way—not an optimum situation for systemwide progress. There are other clear benefits to using collective thinking, including the following:

- Your team develops a sense of community through the process.
- The process brings synergy needed to implement the decisions you make as a result of what you learn along the way.
- You each bring a history, viewpoint, and perspective to the table that enriches the process.

• You begin to build capacity within the system for using data. Don't underestimate the value of building system capacity. You will find that it brings both tangible and intangible benefits that grow over time.

A cooperative-learning maxim says, "No one of us is as smart as all of us." This speaks to the importance of teams looking at data, thinking about data, and considering what to do when they determine what the data really mean. Some districts go beyond having one team to look at data to having a different team for various areas in the district or school. Each team develops expertise and experience in a particular area, looks at data from that perspective, and then shares its knowledge and insights with others in the district and school. Four areas in which schools or districts might consider forming teams are (a) curriculum, (b) instruction, (c) assessment, and (d) research. Each team studies the data from that aspect and brings that perspective to the table.

The Curriculum Data Work Team for the Southside School District had been hard at work since they received the scores on the state test. Their task was to examine the data through the lens of the district's curriculum, with an eye toward using the data from the test reports to recommend improvements in the district's curriculum. Of course, the team had expert knowledge of the district's curriculum in the first place, or this work would not have been possible. The test report was broken down by state standards, so the team was focusing its work on the students' mastery of each state standard. For each grade level and subject area, the team developed a chart showing the mastery levels of the standards, with recommendations for the focus of the curriculum work for the new school year.

After the team finished the immediate task of determining the focus for curriculum work for the next year based on areas where students didn't master standards on the test, the team decided to step back and look at the big picture of curriculum once again. How did curriculum and state testing fit together? What data did the team need to collect to help the district continue to develop its curriculum?

What other questions would you have the team members ask about the data? How would you use the information they put together at the campus level? What other expert teams would you set up to examine the data? What questions would you have them ask about the data?

MANAGING YOUR PROCESS

The process of developing your road map takes time and energy. You will create and carry three sets of information with you on your journey: a data notebook, a master data directory, and an information-based decision-making road map. The first important tool that you will create is your data notebook. The process of developing your road map will generate a number of forms, agendas, and notes. You will keep these in your data notebook.

We are not suggesting that you write all your data in some spiral-bound throwback from your middle-school days. Rather you might compile your data notebook or data folder on your computer. Include in the notebook all the forms you complete, notes from every team meeting, the decisions you make, the timeline for their implementation, and who will implement each decision. Date each document and list the people present at the meeting, along with those who completed the information on each form.

One of the lessons we've learned is that keeping a clear written record is a key to success. Yes, we learned it the hard way. Like the old adage says, "Learn from the mistakes of others. Life is too short to make them all yourself."

Your data notebook will help keep you from taking the same false turn a second (or third or fourth or fifth) time. You will also be able to leave it for those who will follow the path you have created.

AGGREGATION OR DISAGGREGATION?

Sometimes, you will want to look at various aspects of your data as a whole, e.g., the percent of students in your district who scored in the highest category on a standardized test. When you look at the data this way you are collecting all the various pieces into a whole. You are aggregating the data.

At other times, you might want to look at one, or a few, distinct groups of students. In that case, you are taking the collected whole and dividing it into parts. Then you are disaggregating the data. Disaggregated data break the total student population into identified student groups and look at the scores, or whatever you are measuring, by an identified student group instead of the total student population.

Disaggregating data simply means taking the data apart by some identified factor. When you disaggregate, you dig more deeply into the data. This helps you highlight issues that might be common to a group of students. Traditionally, schools have disaggregated student data by gender, race/ethnicity, and socioeconomic status. Under the recently enacted No Child Left Behind Act, districts will also look at groups of students by their English proficiency status and disability status.

Many of the questions you will want to answer will involve disaggregating your data. You can group the scores on any test into identifiable student groups—when you do that, you have disaggregated the data. You can then compare the scores to see if there is some commonality among students in the identified groups or some difference among the identified groups. Disaggregation will expose gaps in student achievement among student groups if gaps exist in your school or district.

For example, one elementary principal was concerned about the reading achievement of third-grade students. When the team disaggregated the data, they discovered that the African American males had the lowest scores. After researching possible strategies, they implemented several reading interventions that were designed specifically for African American males beginning in first grade and continuing through the elementary grades. The students' reading achievement improved.

Data disaggregation is one of the keys to using data to make decisions. We cannot overemphasize the importance of data disaggregation. If you use only aggregate data you run the risk of masking problems and skewing reality. This is as true in a class and a grade level as it is in a school and a district. One size rarely fits all.

You can disaggregate by any factor that gives you an identifiable group of students. You might disaggregate and analyze differences in student achievement by the differences in their teachers' credentials, amount or type of staff development, or years of experience. You can disaggregate and analyze differences in student achievement by looking at the courses students have taken and when—for example, Algebra I in middle school or foreign language in elementary school. You might disaggregate and analyze differences in student achievement by other characteristics, such as the sample list that follows:

- grade level
- length of enrollment in the district
- participation in extracurricular/cocurricular classes
- performance level score on a test
- school the student attends within the district
- socioeconomic status (using free/reduced/paid lunch or parents' educational level)
- special program participation

In short, you can disaggregate and analyze data for any group that you can identify based on a common factor.

WHAT QUESTIONS CAN YOU ANSWER USING DATA ANALYSIS?

Many of us find ourselves at our destination without having planned our route. That method works if you don't care where you're going or if you have plenty of time and resources to waste should you get lost along the way. Since we know you do care and that your resources are not unlimited, when it comes to student learning, remember that the questions you ask should drive everything else you do.

Take some time to think about the questions you will ask, how you can get the answers, and how you will use the answers in your decision-making. This section is designed to guide you through the questions you will ask—the first step in developing your road map.

The first thing to do is to separate the questions you need to answer from the questions you'd like to answer. We encourage you to clearly distinguish between those two types of questions. The need-to-answer questions will clearly relate to your goals, while the nice-to-answer questions will sound like this: "Wouldn't it be interesting to know . . . ?" We distinguish between the two, because it is easy to get caught up in the excitement of looking at data for data's sake. If you do that, you can have lots of nifty numbers and not much information for making your important decisions.

While you may eventually answer some of the questions in the like-to-answer column, the questions you need to answer have to be your first priority. Those answers will help you determine whether you are meeting your goals and help you find the leverage points for improvement. We urge you to begin with information you truly need to know based on your goals. If your system is built correctly, you will be able to add other types of data when you need to answer additional questions.

If you begin with gathering data rather than with developing your questions, you can quickly become overwhelmed. It's easy to lose your sense of direction in a sea of data.

The first questions you need to answer will come from your goals. Sit down with your goals and look at them through this filter: What questions will help you determine whether you are meeting your goals?

Many times you will have goals in the four main areas of (a) student achievement, (b) attendance, (c) discipline, and (d) participation in school activities. We'll use sample questions in these areas, since these areas are commonly accepted as important to student success. They are also commonly found among many schools' and districts' goals. Use our sample questions to start your thinking. Refer to your goals to develop your own specific questions.

WHAT ARE SOME QUESTIONS THAT YOU MIGHT ASK?

What Questions Do Teachers and Principals Ask about Individual Students?

Teachers and principals routinely ask questions about individual students. Teachers and principals can analyze data to answer their questions, get a more complete picture of achievement, and gain insights into student performance. Considering historical information, including information in the cumulative records, contacting former teachers and parents for information, and connecting various sources of information about a student can help teachers and principals better understand and help a student.

Some questions that teachers and principals might ask about an individual student include the following, as the teacher or principal considers, "What is this child's history of achievement, attendance, discipline, and participation?"

Achievement
- What classes has this child taken and what grades did he make in those classes?

- In which special programs did this child take part?
- How do this student's grades compare with his standardized test scores?
- How do this student's grades in one subject compare with his grades in another?
- What are my end-of-year goals for this student, and how is the student progressing toward mastering them?
- How well is this student mastering the objectives of a specific curriculum?

Attendance
- How many days has this child been absent? Why?
- What is this child's historic pattern of attendance?
- How many days has this child been tardy? Why?
- Is the child absent on a certain day each week (such as Monday or Friday)?

Discipline
- How many discipline referrals does this child have? For what reasons?
- Are discipline problems escalating or de-escalating?
- Is this child having discipline problems with certain other students?
- Is this child having discipline problems in other teachers' classes?
- What were this child's discipline problems in other years?

Participation
- In which extracurricular or cocurricular activities does this child participate?
- Does the child belong to noncurriculum-related clubs which meet at school?
- Does the child hold an office in any school organizations?

What Questions Do Principals and Teachers Ask about Groups of Students?

Principals routinely evaluate the performance of groups of students. Teachers, however, tend to evaluate individual student performance while sometimes failing to consider the performance of the class as a whole and student groups within the class. Schmoker (1996) compares this practice "to a grounds keeper managing one section of a lawn" (p. 37). A teacher's focus on evaluating the performance of only one child may also lead to excuses and justifications: "None of Richard's siblings were good at math so there's really no point in trying to make him learn any more than he has already."

When teachers broaden their perspective to focus on patterns within the class, the real power of data analysis becomes clear. At that point teachers no longer see just individual students who need their help, they begin to see patterns of achievement, attendance, discipline, and participation in their classroom. Teachers can then begin to adjust content, instructional methods, classroom management methods, and communication methods, as well as other systems within their classrooms. This approach impacts the achievement of students even more than helping one student at a time with specific problems.

The following questions can help teachers focus on patterns within the class, while helping principals focus on patterns of groups of students within the school:

Achievement
- Are there gaps in achievement among identified student groups? If so, have these gaps changed over time?
- Do students master some subjects better than others?
- Is there a pattern of achievement in groups of students who are in a particular program?
- Which objectives do students master most easily?
- Which objectives do students fail to master?

Attendance
- Is attendance better on some days than others?
- Is attendance better at some times of the year than at other times?
- Is attendance better among some student groups in the class or school than others?
- Is attendance better in some sections or classes than others?
- Is tardiness less of a problem in some sections or classes than others?
- Are some student groups tardy more than other student groups?

Discipline
- What is the pattern of discipline problems in a class? In the school?
- Which student groups are involved in which types of discipline problems?
- What time of day are discipline problems occurring?

- Where (e.g., cafeteria, playground, bus) do discipline problems occur?

Participation

- Which groups of students are involved in what kinds of extracurricular and cocurricular activities?
- What are the grades of students who are involved in each type of extracurricular and cocurricular activity?
- What are the grades of students who are not involved in any type of extracurricular or cocurricular activity?
- What are the discipline referrals of students who are involved in extracurricular and cocurricular activities? Of the students who are not involved in extracurricular and cocurricular activities?
- What is the attendance of students who are involved in extracurricular and cocurricular activities? Of the students who are not involved in extracurricular and cocurricular activities?

What Questions Do Principals Ask about Schools?

The principal is responsible for the overall instructional program of the school, along with oversight for student attendance, discipline, and participation. Therefore, the principal must analyze data to have information to make decisions about every aspect of the school. The principal must also make recommendations to the superintendent and school board regarding decisions they will make about the school. In doing so, the principal looks beyond the categories we've defined previously. For that reason, we've added three categories—big picture, efficiency, and intersection.

The big picture category looks at the overall accomplishment of the school's goals. Looking at the big picture is looking at the whole map—the possible starting points, the possible destinations, the optional routes.

Efficiency is a category that considers the cost and the benefit of choices the school is making. What is the shortest, most direct, resource-savvy way to get where you need to go?

Intersection means that categories begin to cross as you ask questions that extend through more than one category—for example, "Do students who attend school every day get better grades?" or "Do students who have a certain kind of discipline referral have lower grades?" Two, three, or even four categories may intersect and give detailed and valuable disaggregated information.

Of course, teachers often ask big picture, efficiency, and intersection questions, too.

A list of questions by category follows:

Big Picture
- How well is this school reaching our vision, mission, and purpose?
- How well are our students mastering the school's curriculum?
- Are the instructional practices/programs used in this school reaching their goals?
- What do we need to change so that all students master the standards?
- Are there red flags signaling to teachers that certain groups of children may be at risk for failure, so that proactive interventions can be implemented?
- Are parents satisfied with the school's communication about their child's progress and needs?

Efficiency
- What are the financial costs of the instructional practices/programs in this school?
- Are our practices/programs cost-effective?
- Do we have the resources—time, people, technology, and tools—necessary to reach our goals?

Intersection
- How do students' state test scores compare with their semester/end-of-year grades?
- Do students who attend school every day get better grades?
- Do students who have a certain kind of discipline referral have lower grades?
- Do students who are enrolled in certain programs have better grades on standardized tests?
- Do students who have teachers with certain kinds of training have better grades on standardized tests?
- Which program is making the biggest difference increasing student achievement for students who are at-risk? Among students who are in the top 25 percent of achievement? Among the students who are in the middle 50 percent?

- Do student groups report differences in what they like best about the school? What they would like to improve in the school?
- Is there a relationship between student attendance and reading level?
- How do teaching methods impact the students' mastery of the standards?

Achievement
- Which students are mastering the standards by the end of each grade level? Which students are not? Are these students in identifiable groups?
- Have the students who are performing at higher levels now always performed at higher levels? Is the same true for students who are performing at low levels?
- Which students are in the bottom quartile of achievement in this school?
- Which students are in the top quartile of achievement in this school?
- Are there gaps in achievement between identified student groups in this school?
- Are there grade levels that have increases or decreases in student achievement in this school?

- Are there differences in achievement in the subjects taught in this school?
- What is the amount of value added in each teacher's classroom in this school? In each grade level or subject area?

Attendance

- What are the patterns of absenteeism in the school?
- Are there identifiable patterns by grade level and student groups?
- What is the pattern of tardiness in this school?
- Are there identifiable patterns by grade level and student groups?

Discipline

- What are the patterns of student discipline in this school?
- Are there identifiable patterns by student groups?
- Are there identifiable patterns by time of day?
- Are there identifiable patterns by subject area or grade level?
- Are there identifiable patterns by teacher?
- Do some interventions result in fewer repeat referrals than others?

Participation

- What is the pattern of student participation in extracurricular and cocurricular activities in this school?
- Are there some student groups that are overrepresented or underrepresented in some extracurricular or cocurricular activities?
- Are there differences in attendance in groups of students who are involved in extracurricular and cocurricular activities?
- Are there differences in discipline referrals in groups of students who are involved in extracurricular and cocurricular activities?
- When you compare the achievement of groups of students who are in extracurricular and cocurricular activities with students who are not in these activities, are there differences by student group?
- When you compare the attendance of groups of students who are in extracurricular and cocurricular activities with groups of students who are not in these activities, are there differences by student group?
- When you compare the discipline referrals of groups of students who are in extracurricular and cocurricular activities with groups of students who are not in these activities, are there differences by student group?

The problem you see might not be the real problem. When you first look at data, you might be tempted to jump to conclusions and judgments. Although this may be the most exercise you get all day, don't. The data tell only one part of the story. They give you a foundation to ask questions about specific circumstances.

In looking at the data, the central office reading coordinator, Mr. Masenhall, noticed that at Cloudy Point Elementary School the children in Mrs. McDaniel's third-grade class consistently scored lower on the end-of-year reading assessment than the students in any other third-grade class in the school. This had been true for at least the last three years, the years for which Mr. Masenhall had data. Mr. Masenhall went to Cloudy Point to visit with the principal, Mr. Woolvy to discuss whether there was a problem in Mrs. McDaniel's class.

Mr. Woolvy knew immediately what was happening. He knew that Mrs. McDaniel was an excellent reading teacher. For that reason, he placed the students who had the lowest second-grade reading scores in her class. Many of these students entered third grade reading on a primer level. While Mrs. McDaniel was able to bring them a long way in reading, some were still not quite on grade level by the end of third grade.

Learning of the characteristics of the students in Mrs. McDaniel's class led to a discussion of "value added." Mr. Masenhall and Mr. Woolvy decided to look at the data in a different way. They measured the value added per teacher by comparing the end-of-year second-grade reading scores with the end-of-year third-grade scores by teacher for each class in the school, matching data student-by-student. When they did this, they found that Mrs. McDaniel's class showed the greatest gains of any class in the Cloudy Point Elementary School for all three years.

Because of the gains in reading achievement she was able to consistently obtain for her students, Mrs. McDaniel was asked to become a facilitator of professional development in reading for teachers who were teaching primary age students reading below grade level in the district. She also put together a guidebook of teaching strategies and suggestions for other teachers to use.

Are there other data it would be valuable to collect? Are there other ways to look at the data to help get a complete picture? What other cautions about looking beyond the data could you suggest?

What Questions Do Program Directors Ask about Programs?

The questions that a program director will ask about programs depend directly on the goals of the program. Program directors may also find it valuable to ask some of the same questions that teachers and principals ask.

The list for program directors to consider includes the following program-specific questions:

- How well does this program achieve its goals?
- How does the cost of this program compare with the costs of similar programs?
- Is this program cost-effective?
- Have achieved results continued over time?
- How does the achievement of students who are in this program compare with the achievement of students who are not in the program?
- Do some student groups achieve the goals of this program better than other student groups achieve the goals of the program?

What Questions Do Superintendents and Boards of Trustees Ask about School Districts?

Superintendents and boards of trustees have the responsibility of leading the entire system toward improvement. Therefore, they take the information about all areas of the district and use that information to make decisions that impact the whole. For this reason we have added a systems category to this section. Superintendents and boards of trustees also use information from all the other categories we discussed earlier by asking questions about the district, rather than about a specific school or classroom. We've included some examples under achievement, following the section on systems.

Systems
- Do specific types of professional development lead to improvement in student achievement?
- Which programs are the most successful for students in this district?
- Are most parents satisfied with the rate of progress and level of performance of their children in this district?
- Are most parents satisfied with the content and work ethic that are being taught in this district?
- Do most parents believe their children are safe in the schools in this district?
- Are the schools in this district safe as measured by objective measures?

Achievement
- Are there gaps in student achievement among identified student groups in this district?
- Are there grade levels that have increases or decreases in student achievement in this district?
- Are there differences in achievement among the subjects taught in this district?
- Are there differences in achievement among the schools in this district?
- Are there differences in achievement among the feeder patterns in this district?
- What characteristics do students who drop out have in common?
- What characteristics do students who succeed have in common?
- What is the percentage of students who choose to pursue postsecondary education who qualify to attend the institution of their choice?
- What is the percentage of students who choose to pursue employment after high school graduation who are evaluated by their employers as competent entry-level employees?

When you ask your questions, remember the following key points:

1. Begin with your goals.
2. Ask questions that will help you determine whether you are meeting your goals.
3. Ask questions about identified student groups to get the best and most helpful information (disaggregated data).

Worksheet 2.1 gives you a form to answer questions in each of the categories in this section. In addition, you may add any categories that relate to your own goals. As you write your questions, you may also indicate the type of information you are seeking—achievement, attendance, discipline, participation, big picture, efficiency, intersection, and systems. This will help later as you assess your current status and move forward with your data collection and analysis.

Worksheet 2.1
Questions to Answer by Category

Date	
Name	
Goal	
Question	
Question type (circle one): Achievement Attendance Big Picture Discipline	Efficiency Intersection Participation System

The CD contains a template for worksheet 2.1. You may revise the worksheet to fit your needs using standard Word table-editing features.

3

Assessing Your Current Status

If personnel in districts, schools, and classrooms had access to quality data when they need them and knew how to use them, the world of education could look very different from the way it looks today. Dollars could be spent only on effective programs and perhaps students would not fall through the cracks. (Bernhardt 2000a, 3)

So far we've established that everyone who makes decisions in a school district needs to analyze data to inform those decisions. People in different positions sometimes need the same kinds of data and sometimes need different kinds of data. Sometimes they need data presented in the same way, sometimes in different ways—all depending on the questions they are asking. Once again, the question you ask drives the information you need. ◁

We've also suggested that the first step is to determine the questions you will answer. We've suggested that you work as a team and examine your goals to find your first set of questions. We've made suggestions for the types of questions you might ask and have given you a form (worksheet 2.1) for listing your questions. By now you should have a list of questions, the answers to which will help you determine if you are accomplishing the important goals you've set out for your class, school, program, or district.

You're ready for the next step in creating your road map. You are ready to assess your current status. Here's where you're going to determine the data you will gather to answer your questions.

WHAT WILL IT TAKE TO ANSWER YOUR QUESTIONS?

In this section, you can use worksheet 3.1 to record specific details necessary to determine what it will take to answer your questions. First, take the list of questions that you have generated. Ask yourself the following questions about each question on your list. These questions are also on worksheet 3.1 on the CD.

1. Can we currently answer the question?
2. What data do we need so that we can answer the question?
3. Are the data available in our district or school or classroom to answer the question?
4. Where are the data stored?
5. How (in what format) are the data stored?

6. For what years do we have the data?
7. Who collects the data?
8. Does more than one person or department collect the data?
9. How much time, staffing, and energy does it take to obtain the data to answer the question?
10. Are the data clean and accurate?
11. If not, what has to be done to make them clean and accurate?
12. If we don't have the data to answer the question, are the data available somewhere else inside our district? Outside our district?
13. If the data are not available, how can we collect them?

If a question will require you to collect multiple sets of data, you may find it easier to complete a separate worksheet 3.1 for each data set you need to collect.

As you complete the worksheet for a question, you may realize you can't come up with all the answers on the first try. Keep the worksheets and work with your team to find the answers. The answers to these questions form the basis for having the data you need to inform your decisions and for designing a data-analysis system that will be easy for you to use in the future.

The worksheet 3.1 template on the CD includes these questions and space for other questions that you might decide to add as you begin to consider your data. You may revise worksheet 3.1 to fit your needs using standard Word table-editing features.

At this point, pause, catch your breath, and look at what you've done so far. It's time to do a double check. Go back to your goals. Then go back to worksheet 2.1 Ask yourself, "Have we asked the best questions we can ask about our goals?"

We can't say this enough—the power of your data collection and analysis system is in the questions you ask! Before you start collecting data, review your questions on worksheet 2.1 once more. Be sure that you've asked the best questions you can ask at this time.

Next, ask yourself, "Do you know the data you'll gather to answer your questions?" Review your data questions on worksheet 3.1 once more.

When you have your goal stated, your question clear, and your data defined on worksheet 3.1, then you are ready to collect and organize the data for use in your decision-making. When you are ready to collect the data,

Worksheet 3.1
What Will It Take to Answer Our Question?

Date
Name
Goal
Question (from worksheet 2.1)
Can we currently answer the question?
What data do we need?
Are the data available in our district?
Where are the data stored?
In what format are the data stored?
For what years do we have the data?
Who collects the data?
Does more than one person/dept. collect it?
How long does it take to get the data?
Are the data clean and accurate?
What has to be done to clean the data?
Are the data available somewhere else?
If not available, can we collect them?

following the checklist in worksheet 3.2 will help assure that the organization process goes smoothly.

Worksheet 3.2 is designed to help with the collection of your data. Answer the following questions about the data to collect:

- What is the purpose of the data collection?
- What data are to be collected?
- Who is to collect the data?
- Where are the data to be collected?
- What form are the data in?
- For what years are the data to be collected?
- Who are the data to be given to?
- What is the deadline for the collection to be complete?

Worksheet 3.2 will help those who are going to collect data understand the purpose for which they are collecting the data, the form in which the data is needed, the timeline for collection, the importance of the data's accuracy, and the person to whom the data must be given. Once you've completed the worksheet, share it with everyone involved in the project. Better yet, have the key team members help you complete the worksheet so that everyone knows their responsibilities and understands the importance of their contributions from the very beginning of the project.

The worksheet 3.2 template on the CD includes this checklist and space for other items you might decide to add as your team makes the worksheet. You may revise worksheet 3.2 to fit your needs using standard Word table-editing features.

What Did You Find?

At this point you have asked important questions based on your goals. You have determined the data you need to collect and you have completed a worksheet that tells you where your data are and what condition your data are in. Now it is time to determine what you can do with your data immediately and what projects may have to be delayed until data can be input or cleansed. Once you have those answers, you may want to skip ahead to another part of this book. For all you first-born children, that is fine with us. You do not have to read every page in order; we want you to

Worksheet 3.2
Data Collection Checklist

Name
Date
Goal
Question
What is the purpose of the data collection?
What data are to be collected?
Who will collect the data?
Where are the data to be collected?
What form are the data in?
For what years are the data to be collected?
Who are the data to be given to?
What is the deadline for the collection?

see this as a "choose your own adventure" book from here on out. For all you last-born babies of the family, it's time to quit coloring in the margins.

You will probably find yourself in one of the following places:

1. You have asked a question, you have the data to answer it, and you can sit down right now to analyze your data and answer the question. You can do this without even a computer program, much less a data warehouse. This sort of thing usually happens when your question involves a single student or a few students with a small number of data points to consider. This is great! You are ready to go to the next step in the process of developing your road map. If you are at this point, you can answer your question.

2. You have the data you need to answer your question. Your data are in a usable format. You have an efficient and easy-to-use data analysis system that has the data in it and enables you to answer your question. Congratulations! You are well on the road to developing your road map. In fact, you can skip ahead to part 2.

Part 2 guides you as you take the data you have and turn them into information for decision-making. Later you will want to visit chapter 4 to consider the big picture of data collection—to look at your data sources and develop your district or campus master data directory as your resource for other questions you plan to ask.

3. You have your question, you tried to fill in the worksheet 3.1, but you don't have what you need to answer your question. You are probably fairly frustrated. The simple act of attempting to fill in the data worksheet for a few questions tells you very quickly whether the current process of data collection and storage in your school and district works for you.

If you are here, you know that you have some important questions. You know you can't answer them because you either don't have the data to answer them or you have the data, but they don't help you because they aren't accurate or complete or in a usable format. Maybe you can't find the data. In any case, the next step is to go through the process of determining and recording the data you do have. Then you will be able to see what you are missing. After that you can develop a system to collect the missing data.

Chapter 4 gives the step-by-step process of going through all the data in your district to determine what you currently have to develop your master data directory. The added benefit of developing your district or cam-

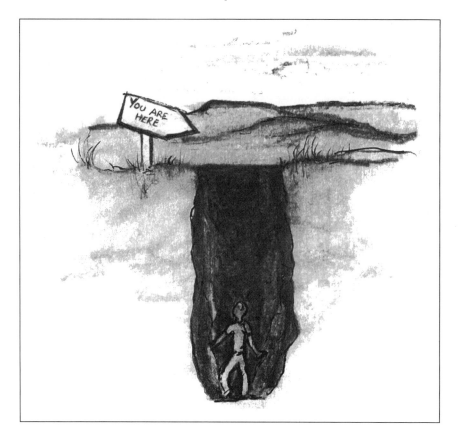

pus master data directory is that you will have it as your resource for other questions you ask in the future.

4. You have your question, you filled in the worksheet completely, you have all the data you need to answer the question, but you realize that you don't have enough long rulers, yellow highlighters, and legal pads—not to mention hours in the day or days in the week—to do the computations required to analyze the data to answer your question. Theoretically, you can analyze the data you have, but you will have to give up sleeping, eating, and other similar luxuries. In short, you find yourself faced with a complicated data analysis problem but without a data analysis system. Your heart sinks at the prospect. Our hearts sank at the prospect—we've been there. We don't like it there. We do not want to go back.

You are not in a good place. You have a difficult choice to make. As we see it, you have two options. If your only choice is to use long rulers, highlighters, calculators, or spreadsheets for complex data analysis, then our advice is to be very careful when you pick the goals you will ask questions about and the questions you ask.

Finding the answer to each question will be slow going. Be prudent and ask only the most important questions, the ones that are crucial to inform your decisions. Ask only the questions that are worth the time you or your staff will have to invest. Determine the time it will take to analyze the data before you begin and ask yourself, "Knowing that it will take 25 staff-hours to analyze this data, will the information I gain be worth the time investment?" This is a classic cost/benefit or return-on-investment analysis. Make sure the prize is worth the race.

> **Here is Edward Bear, coming downstairs now, bump, bump, bump, on the back of his head behind Christopher Robin. It is, as far as he knows, the only way of coming downstairs, but sometimes he feels there really is another way, if only he could stop bumping for a moment and think of it. (A. A. Milne 1926)**

Your other choice is to consider investing in a data-analysis system, so that you can avoid the need to severely limit the questions you wish to pose. Just a few years ago, data-analysis systems cost hundreds of thousands of dollars, a price that was certainly out of the range for nearly all small to medium-size school districts. Now data-analysis systems are priced much more reasonably, giving even a small district the opportunity to consider having technology do the hours of analysis so that the people can spend their time making the decisions, not doing the math.

To return to a portion of the Deming quote that inspired this handbook, "Improvement is possible and essential. The development of human beings by using the talent they bring to their work cannot help but result in improvement" (Schmoker and Wilson 1993, 8). Allowing people to use their time and talents to make decisions will improve our schools and districts. Making them spend hours and hours doing calculations probably won't. Our talents need to be used making and implementing decisions for the good of our students, based on information we can easily access.

If you decide to consider a data-analysis system, be sure you read chapter 5, where we've included critical aspects that will help you in making your decision.

Without accurate data, people make assumptions that are inaccurate and sometimes damaging. Having a data-analysis system enables you to accurately answer important questions.

In Manchester School District, teachers kept telling Mr. Downs, the new superintendent, that they thought it was better to retain more students than the district was currently retaining. This message was loudest from high school teachers, who insisted that a significant number of students simply weren't ready for high school, and, therefore, must have been socially promoted throughout the lower grades. Mr. Downs had read the research about retention, which indicated that retention could increase a student's chances to drop out of high school. So he wanted to answer the questions, "Have the current high school students been promoted, or placed in the next grade, or retained in prior years?" "How many students have we retained each year?" and "What has happened to the students who were retained?" Mr. Downs thought the questions would be easy to answer. However, the process of answering the questions was so labor-, time-, and energy-intensive that it caused Mr. Downs to begin the search for a data warehouse and data-analysis tool.

The handwritten lists that principals kept each year were the only record of student retentions in the district. The only way to determine what happened to the students who had been retained was to take a name off the list and compare it with the current year's student database, one name at a time. If it wasn't in the current database, the next option was to go to last year's yearbook, since the student database renewed itself yearly and old data were stored in a way that made them very difficult to restore. Then the superintendent still had to find a way to learn where students were who did not appear on the current year's database or in the yearbook.

Staff found the answer to the question, "How many students have we retained each year" by counting the number of names on each principal's handwritten list and adding the numbers. The number was surprising. The current high school students did not represent a group of students who had been socially promoted; in fact, between one-fourth and one-third of them had been retained each year in the primary grades. The answers to both questions were important to learn—but gathering the data by hand was incredibly labor-intensive and time consuming.

In what instances have you made assumptions, then learned those assumptions weren't valid when you analyzed data? In what cases have you wanted to answer a question, but found that analyzing the data was too difficult?

If you are like we were, then you have a lot of data, but you don't have the right kind, or what you have isn't where you need it. You may have some data that are ready to use, some data that can be made ready to use, and some data that are missing altogether. You may have some data that are inaccurate, and some data that you think you have but can't find or that you think is accurate but in fact isn't. You may find that to answer your questions, you need some data that you never dreamed of collecting.

Data, data everywhere and not a thought to think. (Popham 2000)

If you look at your data collection worksheet and find that it has big holes and inconsistencies, if your team gives you a collective "stuffed Teddy Bear look" when you ask, "Now, what do we have and where is it?"—take a deep breath. Do not despair! Soldier on! All is not lost! We have been in that place.

We had big gaps and holes in our data and our knowledge. We had volumes and volumes of data, but no efficient system for managing them, accessing them, or using them. Until we started writing down our questions and the sources of data to answer the questions, we weren't even sure what we had and what we didn't have.

We've learned since then that the way to make sense of all that data is by developing your road map. But we didn't know that at the time. The problem isn't that you don't have data. The problem is that you don't have the map to take you through your data to your destination. As you develop your map, the path will become clear.

4

Thinking about the Data You Have

Collecting data without purpose is meaningless. (Creighton 2001b, 11)

Most school systems have tons of data. In most systems data are collected by a variety of people, stored in a variety of places, set up in a variety of formats, rarely compared, often duplicated, and used very little for decision-making. In most school systems there is no data master list or unified data system.

In chapter 4 we'll help you organize and make sense of all the data that you have hidden around the school or district within your master data directory. The master data directory is the second tool you'll take with you on your journey. As with the data notebook, it will likely be a folder on your computer. It will contain a set of forms that detail the data you have available in your district by type, format, site, and person or department who has the data.

Your master data directory is an important tool for helping you determine the data you have, so that you can also determine the data you need to collect. It will also help you determine if you have duplicate data and efficient collection systems. In addition it will serve as a reference guide so that you and your team will be able to actually find the data you want when you need them without having to scavenge the district late at night with flashlights hunting for the last shoebox of data tapes with test scores from two years ago that someone misplaced.

While we asked you to start with a small number of questions about your current goals, you probably didn't stop there. Using data to inform decisions is a vital part of the continuous improvement process. Therefore, it's important to think about more than just the few questions you are currently asking. Unless you are going to ask only one or two straightforward questions that use a few bits of data to answer, capturing a directory of all the data sources you have available will be invaluable in the long run.

Your master data directory will help you answer both current and future questions. The best way to develop your master data directory is to gather your team back together.

We've approached the wealth of data that you have to consider from four viewpoints:

- What types of data do you have?
- How are the data formatted?
- Where are the data stored?
- Who has the data?

Looking at data through these four lenses gives four different pictures that will enable you to find all the data that you have in your district. Leave one out and you will invariably fail to remember or discover some data currently somewhere in your district and that could be critical to your quest.

WHAT TYPES OF DATA DO YOU HAVE?

You have data. You have lots of data. But do you really know what you have?

While there are a number of ways to categorize data, we have used the following three categories: contextual indicators, process indicators, and outcome indicators, as recommended by Sandifer (1999, 1).

Contextual indicators describe the conditions of the students, teachers, schools, and community. These indicators influence the process and outcome indicators. Contextual indicators are helpful in interpreting educational processes and outcomes in the district and school. Many of the contextual indicators are the same as demographic indicators. Other contextual indicators include school climate and building conditions. Together these form the framework within which your students learn.

The organization largely controls the process indicators. The district may operate on an elementary, middle, or high school model or on a primary, elementary, junior high, or high school model. Students may take a foreign language in third grade; teachers may be required to use a specific instructional approach when they teach reading. Process indicators are places the school system can impact to change results.

Outcome indicators are the results the system obtains. These indicators are used to measure the system. How many of your students scored at the proficient level on the latest standardized test? How many of your high school graduates pursue higher education? What effect does being in your school system have on your students' learning? These are outcome indicators.

You probably have a lot of contextual demographic data on your students. Worksheet 4.1 has the form to record the contextual data you currently have available. It also has spaces for you to add other contextual data that you have or plan to collect. Following is a list of contextual data that you might have or decide you will collect to use in data disaggregation.

Worksheet 4.1
Contextual Data Collection

Name:
Date:

Contextual Indicator	Currently Collect (yes or no)	Plan to Collect (yes or no)
Student Name		
Student Date of Birth		
Student Enrollment Date		
Student Ethnicity		
Student Gender		
Student Identification Number		
Student Mobility		
Student Mode of Transportation to School		
Student Socioeconomic Status		

Contextual indicators on students include the following:

- name
- date of birth
- enrollment date/withdrawal date
- ethnicity
- gender
- identification number
- address
- home language
- mobility
- method of transportation to/from school
- socioeconomic status (as determined by free/reduced/paid lunch status or other objective indicator)
- disability

A Word about Confidentiality

In gathering data and using information, especially contextual information, you must comply with laws regarding confidentiality. Just because something can be reported doesn't mean that it is legal to report it.

Specific regulations that schools and districts are required to follow include the Family Educational Rights and Privacy Act (FERPA) 20 U.S.C. § 1232g; 34 CFR Part 99, and your state laws regarding open records, employee files, and confidentiality.

FERPA

FERPA regulations protect the identity of individual students. That protection may have an impact on the way schools and districts release aggregated and disaggregated data. For you to release information about a student group that group must be large enough so that no individual child is identifiable. For example, if you report that fifth-grade Hispanic males scored at the 60th percentile on a recent test given in Ms. Wixon's fifth-grade class, and Ms. Wixon has one Hispanic male in her class, that child is easily identifiable and you are in violation of FERPA. If you need additional information, the U.S. Department of Education website has a division for FERPA at www.ed.gov/offices/OII/fpco/ferpa/.

National School Lunch Act (NSLA)

In a Joint Letter about the Use of Student Information Collected Pursuant to the National School Lunch Program written December 17, 2002, the U.S. Departments of Education and Agriculture clarified policies regarding schools' collection and use of confidential student lunch information as follows:

> Section 9 of the Richard B. Russell National School Lunch Act (NSLA) establishes requirements and limitations regarding the release of information about children certified for free and reduced-price meals provided under the National School Lunch Program. The NSLA allows school officials responsible for determining free and reduced-price meal eligibility to disclose aggregate information about children certified for free and reduced-price school meals. Additionally, the statute permits determining officials to disclose the names of individual children certified for free and reduced-price school meals and the child's eligibility status (whether certified for free meals or reduced-price meals) to persons directly connected with the administration or enforcement of a federal or state education program. This information may be disclosed without parental consent.
>
> Because Title I is a federal education program, determining officials may disclose a child's eligibility status to persons directly connected with, and who have a need to know, a child's free and reduced-price meal eligibility status to administer and enforce the new Title I requirements. The statute, however, does not allow the disclosure of any other information obtained from the free and reduced-price school meal application or obtained through direct certification. School officials must keep in mind that the intent of the confidentiality provisions in the NSLA is to limit the disclosure of a child's eligibility status to those who have a "need to know" for proper administration and enforcement of a federal education program. As such, we expect schools to establish procedures that limit access to a child's eligibility status to as few individuals as possible.
>
> We urge school officials, prior to their disclosing information on the school lunch program eligibility of individual students, to enter into a memorandum of understanding or other agreement to which all involved parties (including both school lunch administrators and educational officials) would adhere. This agreement would specify the names of the individuals who would have access to the information, how the information would be used in implementing Title I requirements, and how the information would be protected from unauthorized uses and third-party dis-

closures, and would include a statement of the penalties for misuse of the information.

Personnel

As you collect demographic information throughout your system, be sure you know what you can, and cannot, report regarding your employees. In some states, procedures for reporting personnel information might be determined by state law, negotiated agreements, or contractual agreements. In other states, specific laws might not apply, but your attorney may advise you to maintain confidentiality regarding certain items. Some information, such as name, credentials, and years of experience are probably considered open records—but again, your local counsel can advise you on the appropriateness of collecting and storing individually identifiable data elements.

You can make changes in your process indicators and bring about different results. You work on the processes and impact the outcomes. Some processes are easier to work on than others, of course, but all can be impacted in some way by someone.

Worksheet 4.2 has the form to record the process indicators you currently have and the indicators you plan to collect to use in decision-making.

We've included a few examples of process indicators in each category. The categories are common to all schools and districts, while specifics within the categories might vary depending on the individual school or district. Sample process indicators are set out below.

Parent process indicators include the following:

* attendance at parent/teacher conferences
* level of parent involvement in school events

Program process indicators include the following:

* class size
* pilot/innovative program participation
* special education instructional delivery model
* programs offered for exceptional students (e.g., gifted/talented, special education, targeted reading programs, advanced placement)

Worksheet 4.2
Process Data Collection

Name:
Date:

Parent Indicators:	Currently Collect (yes or no)	Plan to Collect (yes or no)
Program Indicators:	Currently Collect (yes or no)	Plan to Collect (yes or no)
Student Indicators:	Currently Collect (yes or no)	Plan to Collect (yes or no)
Teacher Indicators:	Currently Collect (yes or no)	Plan to Collect (yes or no)

For an individual student, process indicators include both current and past:

- advisor
- attendance
- discipline report
- extracurricular and cocurricular participation
- grade level
- interventions (e.g., tutoring, summer school)
- level of English fluency
- tardiness data
- teacher(s)
- courses

Teacher process indicators include the following:

- attendance
- credentials (e.g., master's degree)
- certification (e.g., elementary or out-of-field/emergency permit)
- number of years experience
- professional development

Finally, let's look where many people start—at the outcome indicators. Often people start—and stop—with standardized test data. As you already know, there's much more to consider than one test score, certainly much more to consider than only outcome indicators.

Worksheet 4.3 has the form to record the outcome indicator data you currently have and the data you plan to collect to use in decision-making.

Outcome indicator data includes the following:

Assessment results
- ACT results
- Advanced Placement Examination results
- assessments from programs such as CCC, Compass, Accelerated Reader, Reading Counts
- authentic assessments (e.g., portfolios, performances, projects, pre-sentations)

Worksheet 4.3
Outcome Indicators Collection

Name:
Date:

Outcome Indicators	Currently Collect (yes or no)	Plan to Collect (yes or no)

- benchmark test results
- criterion-referenced test results
- end-of-course tests
- exit examinations
- local assessments/districtwide assessments
- norm-referenced test results
- PLAN results
- PSAT results
- SAT results
- school aptitude test results
- school readiness assessment results

Data on graduates, including the following:

- number of seniors entering postsecondary education, military, employment
- number of college freshmen taking remedial courses
- high school completion rate/graduation rate
- vocational courses completion rate

Schoolwide records, including the following:

- discipline referrals/student behavior indicators
- dropout rate grades 7–12
- master schedule showing course offerings and number of students in each class
- observations (e.g., graffiti, broken windows)
- participation in advanced placement classes
- participation in extracurricular and cocurricular activities
- promotion rate
- logs from library reading programs (e.g., Accelerated Reader/Reading Counts)
- records of use of math manipulatives
- records of use of science kits
- retention rate

Student self-reports, journals, and logs; interviews with parents, teachers, and students; survey data (teacher/student/parent/community); and teacher-gathered data, including the following:

- classroom observations with checklist
- grades in courses, progress reports, report cards
- individual reading inventory results
- running record results of student reading
- samples of student work
- writing samples

We're pleased to report that, during the last few years we've increased our dependence on using numerical data to make decisions. Before that we were more likely to base decisions on our perceptions—sometimes, perceptions were all we had. Even though we have all this numerical data in formats that we can use, it's important to remember that perceptions still have a place in decision-making. In fact the use of perceptual data is a vital part of decision-making. Victoria Bernhardt has developed a number of excellent instruments and tools to use in measuring perceptions within school environments. Used along with numerical data, perceptions round out the picture and help you understand the actions you might take to improve your schools.

At Windy Way Middle School, the principal, Mrs. Wiznot, prided herself on student safety. She had read the literature that said the number 1 concern of parents was that their children be safe at school. Her school had a school resource officer. It had doors that were locked on the outside. They required visitors to sign in and wear badges. Teachers stood by their classroom doors during class changes. She considered Windy Way to be the epitome of safety.

After learning about using data to make decisions, however, Mrs. Wiznot decided to survey her students about their perceptions of the school's safety. She felt certain that she would get results that would be worthy of a great newspaper article in the local press, if not a magazine article in her state's education journal—"How to Make

Sure Your Students Feel Safe at School." She designed a survey that asked questions about school safety and put the survey on the computers in the school lab.

When each class went to the lab and logged on, the students took the survey. The results were instantly tabulated, then sent to the computer at her desk. By week's end, she had results from all 800 students in the school. She was astonished. The students reported that they felt afraid in the common areas of the school, especially the rest rooms and the dressing rooms. Small groups of students were intimidating other students—and adults didn't know it. Students reported that they responded to the survey because they knew it was anonymous. They were afraid to tell their teachers.

Mrs. Wiznot knew she had to take immediate action. What would she have done if she hadn't asked the students?

What other data could she consider? What areas could you consider for the use of perception data? How could you combine the use of numerical and perception data to make decisions?

HOW ARE YOUR DATA FORMATTED?

Because data come in different formats, it's easy for some data to become lost or misplaced when it is stored. One of the problems we continually find is that schools and districts have data, or at least they used to have data, but they can't find it. Sometimes they can find it but don't know what it is. Maybe the person who put the shoebox full of data tapes in the closet no longer works in the district and no one else has opened the box. So no one knows what is in the box. Or has noticed that the box is in the closet. Or has ever opened the closet door. Or even knows where the closet is. You get the point.

We've included the following list of formats for data along with worksheet 4.4, the form to record your available data by format.

Data are available in the following formats in most school systems:

- compact disk (CD-ROM)
- databases

Worksheet 4.4
Data Format Collection

Name:

Date:

Data Source (check all that apply)	CD	Data-base	Data Disk	Data Tape	Hard Copy	Main Frame	Spread Sheet	State System

- data disk
- data tape
- hard copy
- local information system (mainframe)
- spreadsheets
- state information system (mainframe)

If a necessary data element is only in hard-copy format, someone will have to put the information into digital form for input into a data-analysis system when and if you decide you need the information in the data analysis system.

You can use worksheet 4.4 to record your available data by format. You can also use it to help you determine what you will have to do to data to make them usable, since each format has to be treated in certain ways before it can be entered in a data-analysis system or printed in a hard copy for manual analysis.

WHERE ARE YOUR DATA ELEMENTS LOCATED OR STORED?

Since schools and districts have so much data and usually so little space to store them, they end up putting them in a variety of creative places. Such creativity might get the data well secured, but doesn't necessarily make it easy to find when it's time to use them. For that matter, it doesn't make it easy to even know what is available.

The following list of data storage sites will help you discover the data that is available and where you might find it. Worksheet 4.5 gives a form to record your available data by location.

Data are available in the following places in most school systems:

- compact disk storage containers
- computer hard drives
- desk drawers
- file cabinets
- file folders
- shoeboxes
- storage boxes
- teachers' grade books
- teacher lounges
- restrooms
- automobile trunks (we do not make this stuff up!)

As with the data format information, listing the storage sites on worksheet 4.5 will help you think about data sources you have forgotten. The completed worksheet will also give you a master list of data by site for the master data directory.

WHO HAS THE DATA YOU NEED?

Your data are in a variety of formats, in a number of storage locations, and, we are certain, collected and stored by lots of different people. Some of these people know that other people have data. Some probably do not. Some of them retired two years ago.

The purpose of examining the list of possible "whos" by completing worksheets 4.6, 4.7, and 4.8 is to develop a master list detailing who has what data for you to use now and in the future. Think of the hours you will save by being able to go to one list and find who has the data you need! Not only that, if you determine that some of this data need to be in a data warehouse, then you save even more time by having ready access to the data.

Worksheet 4.5
Data Storage Collection

Name:								
Date:								

Data Source (check all that apply)	CD Container	Computer Hard Drive	Desk Drawer	File Cabinet	File Folder	Shoe-box	Storage Box	Grade Book

We are following the same format for the people and departments as we did for the data formats and the data storage sites. We're giving you a list, along with worksheets 4.6, 4.7, and 4.8 for you to complete. Worksheet 4.6 tracks the campus-based people who have data; worksheets 4.7 and 4.8 list the district-based personnel.

The people who work in the following divisions in your school system may have access to the data you need.

Campus-Based Personnel
- assistant principal's office
- campus data collection office
- campus administrative office
- classrooms
- counselor's office
- health room
- principal's office
- school secretary's office

District-Based Personnel
- business office
- central or district office
- curriculum and instruction office
- data collection and management department
- federal programs office
- food services office
- grants office
- human resources office
- operations department
- public information office
- research office
- resource officer's office
- special education office
- special programs office
- student support office
- superintendent's office
- technology department
- testing department
- transportation department

The list of people, offices, and departments who have access to data in schools and districts is extensive. You can easily understand how data can become lost, duplicated, or simply confused. For data related to some questions, the sources might be more limited. For example, when asking about the number of referrals for student bus discipline, the campus principals and the transportation office are probably the best two places to start in most districts. For questions about numbers of students visiting the

Worksheet 4.6
People/Department Data Collection
Campus-Based Departments
Worksheet 1 of 3

Name:								
Date:								

Data Source (check all that apply)	Asst. Principal	Data Collection Office	Campus Office	Class-rooms	Coun-selor's Office	Nurse's Office	Prin-cipal's Office	Secre-tary's Office

Worksheet 4.7
People/Department Data Collection
District-Based Departments
Worksheet 2 of 3

Name:

Date:

Data Source (check all that apply)	Business Office	District Office	Curriculum/Instruction Office	Data Collection Office	Federal Program's Office	Food Services Office	Grants Office	Human Resources Office	Operations Office

Worksheet 4.8
People/Department Data Collection
District-Based Departments
Worksheet 3 of 3

Name:									

Date:									

Data Source (check all that apply)	Public Information Office	Research Office	Special Education Office	Special Programs Office	Student Support Office	Superintendent's Office	Technology Department	Testing Department	Transportation Department

nurse's office, it would make sense to start with the nurse, or, in a large district, the coordinator of nurses.

As it relates to the big picture of data use within a school or district, however, remember that a wealth of data is available from all these people. Many times we simply don't think about asking. Or coordinating. Or sharing.

Worksheets 4.6, 4.7, and 4.8 are for compiling your data sources by person/department. As with the data format information and the storage site information, listing the people or office or department source information may help you think about data sources you have forgotten. It also provides a master list of data by person/department for your master data directory.

In addition to considering internal sources of data, consider external sources. You may be surprised at the amount of data that is available for your use. These sources include the following:

- *Local government agencies.* City and county governments and local libraries are good sources of information. Consider the information you might glean from voter registration lists, median income information by neighborhood, or housing starts.
- *State Department of Education.* Review the directory of offices for those that may have relevant data. Some offices have data for the state as a whole and for local districts.
- *Intermediate service agencies.* In some states, data are available in educational service centers, county boards of education, specialty agencies, and educational consortia offices.
- *University and college departments of education.* Faculty and students may have completed research studies on some aspect of your district operations. They may also be willing to conduct research for you as part of their course work.
- *Federal agencies.* Browse agencies such as the Department of Education's National Center for Education Statistics at www.nces.ed.gov. or the U.S. Census Bureau at www.census.gov.
- *Regional research centers.* Organizations such as SREB (Southern Regional Education Board) at www.sreb.org or any one of the regional education centers sponsored by the U.S. Department of Education, such as www.nwrel.org/national/index.html, might have data you can use.

At this point, you know your goals and questions you need to answer to determine if you are meeting those goals. You have a good idea of the data you have available in your district and available to you from other sources. You have begun to develop your master data directory, which contains your data sources and lets you know which data are (and are not) ready to be used to answer the questions you have now and questions you will want to ask in the future.

If you can answer your questions with handwritten spreadsheets, yellow pads, and long rulers, then you may want to take your master data directory and go on to chapter 6, Reporting Information. If you are ready to think about using a data-analysis system to answer your questions, then chapter 5 will help you design your system.

5

Designing a Data-Analysis System

Avoid data frenzy. (Adam and Quinn 2002, 1)

In chapter 5 we'll help you design a data-analysis system that enables you to turn data into information efficiently and quickly. If you have only a bit of data to analyze or lots of time and willing staff, you may be fine with the long rulers and sharp pencils. Time and energy are finite resources, however, and, as we said in chapter 3, having a data-analysis system gives you freedom to ask questions without being concerned that you are over-burdening the people who will be up nights putting the numbers together to get the answers you need.

If you are ready to think about data-analysis systems, then this chapter is for you.

WHAT IS DATA ANALYSIS?

Data analysis is the process of turning your data into information that you can use to make decisions.

That explanation of data analysis makes it sound simple. Straw into gold; data into information—poof! In reality, data analysis has a set of components, which, if ignored or not executed correctly, will cause your information to be of limited value. We believe that to turn data into information you have to have some sort of data-analysis system.

If your question is simple enough to take a yellow pad and pencil or a calculator to figure out the answer, then you have the simplest of data-analysis systems. You have your question to answer and your data to be analyzed, you analyze it with pencil and paper and a little brainpower, and you obtain the results of that analysis.

When you get more than a few students, more than a few data elements, and more than a few variables, then you begin to spend significant amounts of time and energy on the computation of the analysis. At that point, using data-analysis technology really pays off.

To answer all but the most rudimentary of questions you will ask about your goals, you will need a data-analysis system that uses technology to manipulate data quickly, accurately, and efficiently. Otherwise you and your staff end up spending time and energy manipulating data, when those resources are better spent asking questions, reporting information, and making decisions.

Defining your data-analysis processes and having written procedures to follow are key components in a data-analysis system. Written procedures are the only way you can maintain the integrity of the process and replicate the process in future data-analysis procedures.

What Are the Components of a Data-Analysis System?

A data-analysis system is made up of parts that must fit seamlessly into one another for the system to maintain efficiency and accuracy in data collection, storage, analysis, and reporting. We definitely intend that the word *system* should encompass more than an organized collection of data. You can organize your data in a disk storage box. To analyze your data, you have to be able to look at them inside out, upside down, from every angle, and often in minute detail. More important, your data elements must be able to relate to each other.

The components of a data-analysis system are:

- data elements
- a process to collect data
- a tool to input data
- a tool to store data

- a tool to analyze data
- a tool to report information

Data Elements

Data consist of discrete elements. Each individual piece of information is one data element (e.g., birth date, math subtest score, student identification number).When you analyze data you are grouping and comparing various data elements with one another by some common factor or factors.

While there are a number of ways to categorize data elements, we use the three categories we first discussed in chapter 4. These three categories are (a) contextual indicators, (b) process indicators, and (c) outcome indicators.

Contextual indicators help define the context or environment in which the school or district operates. These indicators influence the school or district, but are generally not controlled by the school and are generally considered to be beyond the school's ability to change, at least in the short term. Contextual indicators describe the conditions of the students, teachers, schools, and community.

Remember that contextual indicators include demographic elements such as education level of the parents; gender, race or ethnicity; eligibility for free or reduced-price lunch; and language spoken in the home. These indicators influence the process and outcome indicators. Contextual indicator data help you interpret educational processes and outcomes in the classroom, school, and district.

Unlike the "come-as-you-are" contextual indicators, school systems can usually control process indicators. These indicators are where you work to change results. Examples of process indicators include program participation, teacher qualifications, course offerings, instructional methods, and student attendance.

Outcome indicators are the results the system obtains. These indicators are used to measure the system. Examples of outcome indicators include results on any test (norm-referenced, criterion-referenced, teacher-made), graduation rate, number of students attending college, and course grades.

If you have not done so, go back to chapter 4 for the list of samples of each type of indicator and complete the form to record the data you currently have and plan to collect to answer your questions.

Why Are Data Elements Important?

Although we think that question is a lot like asking, "Why are bones important to the human body?" we still feel the need to stress that without data elements you have no need for the other five components. Without data elements you would have nothing to support the other components.

Data elements are the content of your data-analysis system. What goes into your system will define the questions that you will ultimately be able to answer using your data-analysis system. Having the right data elements is the key to making information-based decisions.

Data elements are critically important for two reasons:

1. The value of your data-analysis system will depend on the data you have in it.
2. The accuracy of your information will depend on the accuracy of your data elements.

You simply cannot answer your questions if you don't have the data to generate the answers. That's why we start with the questions, not with data. You can collect all sorts of nifty data and still have absolutely nothing of value when it comes to decision-making.

So, after questions, data elements are the most important parts—without the right data elements, you can't answer your questions.

And what are the right data elements? The ones you need to answer your questions, of course!

The right data elements are also the ones that are accurate. Accurate data is critical to the success of your system. Do we mean your data-analysis system or do we mean your school system? Yes. If you start with inaccurate data elements, you are pretty much doomed from the outset. You are making decisions about children based on bad information generated from bad data elements. That may be worse than not having data to make a decision at all. At least in the latter case, you *know* that you don't know.

Data elements, like atoms, are the building blocks of your system. Separately they are tiny and often insignificant; together they become a formidable force.

A Process to Collect Data

A data-collection process involves gathering the data you need to analyze to answer the questions you want to answer. Note that we used the word process here. This is not a one-time-does-it event. Data collection is an ongoing, carefully defined, clearly documented process. Districts and schools that fail to think in terms of a data-collection process may find themselves doing a good job collecting data the first time, or even the second time. Then one or two years down the road, they realize they forgot to collect an important piece or two of data and the whole system breaks down.

When you consider data collection, think about ways to collect data once and then use them over and over. Efficiency matters. Accuracy matters. Both efficiency and accuracy are compromised every time you have to deal with the same data collected in a different way by a different person. For example, if the clerk who enters attendance data uses the student's name Mary Katherine Smith, and the food service secretary enrolls the student in the food service program as M. Katherine Smith, the two systems may never know that it's the same child. This may not be a problem until you want to answer the question, "Do students who are on free lunch have more absences than students who are on paid lunch?" If you can't match the students, then you can't answer the question. Accuracy has been compromised because two different people entered data at two different places in two different ways, without common protocols for doing so.

In the first section of this handbook, you developed your list of questions to answer. In the second section, you developed the list of sources of data to access to answer your questions. You considered the types of data you have and the places data are stored in your school and district. You thought about the people and departments who may have control of and access to data. You made lists of data to collect to answer your questions. These lists are the basis for your data-collection system.

Some basic data elements will always be collected—these form the first layer of your data-analysis system. We suggest that you consider the following list as your foundation data elements:

- student name
- student identification number (unique to the student)

- ethnicity
- gender
- disability status
- English proficiency
- standardized test scores

Beyond these elements, you'll collect the elements you need to answer your own specific questions. Some of the additional elements might include:

- courses
- schedules
- absences
- extracurricular or cocurricular participation
- benchmark test scores
- discipline referrals
- teacher demographic information

A Tool to Input Data

You have to collect and organize both small and large amounts of data. Of course, the more data you add the more complex the process becomes. Inputting data is where you begin to see a big difference in how you handle small amounts of data and large amounts of data. For small amounts of data, you input the data by writing the numbers and words on a sheet of paper or by entering them in a spreadsheet on your computer. For large amounts of data, you really, really, really need a data warehouse.

Anyone who quips that a data warehouse can be built within a week, or even a month, is either foolish or very naive. We've gotten you this far; we'd hate to lose you to foolishness and naiveté now!

The first major obstacle, and unfortunately one we've seen cause many to turn back in frustration, is that the data in your warehouse must be "clean." You must, must, must be able to rely on the integrity of the data. One of the keys to the value of any data-analysis system is the cleanliness of the data that are in it. Bad data get you bad information. Bad information gets you bad decisions. Put bad decisions based on bad information in front of the public and the school board at an open meeting, and kiss your credibility goodbye.

Cleaning data requires a powerful data-management tool. Doing the job properly and structuring the data properly can be a sanity-challenging task. Importing data isn't where the difficulty lies; you can most certainly load information from your spreadsheets, fixed-width or comma-delimited files, or other databases. The devil is in the details, as you might guess.

When you're building a warehouse, the devil is data validation. What if you discover two students who share the same identification number? Or a handful of student records that contain almost identical information for the same year, but each with different test results? Or what if Mary Katherine Smith is Mary K. Smith in your student information system, but M. Katherine Smith on the CD that contains the state test scores? Is she the same student? Which record is the right record? What if you reused teacher identification numbers when one teacher left and another was hired, but now you want to go back and match the teachers with the courses they taught? These are just a few of the problems to tackle in cleaning the data.

Once you have your data elements and are sure they are correct, you'll need the third element of the data-analysis system—a tool that will input data and will help give the data additional, meaningful structure. Much of the test data that comes to your district is not structured in ways that can be immediately used to make decisions or reported to the public.

For example, many times testing companies send out files that contain scaled test scores. Your district, however, may be required to report those scaled scores according to proficiency levels. Any tool that will be used to input your data must allow you to create ranges from those scaled scores that can be sorted according to the categories that your state or district uses. For example, one state uses basic, proficient, and advanced as the three categories in which test scores are reported. The district takes the scaled scores that come from the test publisher and translates them into the three performance levels for each grade and subject area. If ever there was a task you'd like to let a computer do for you, this has to be it. Theoretically, you could report scaled scores, but if you did, the information wouldn't mean anything to the public, parents, or students.

The kind of data input software we think you absolutely must have in your tool kit is referred to as an ETL (extract, transform, and load) tool. Whether you purchase and use your own data-management tool or contract with a company for that service, make certain the tool can perform the following basic functions:

- Import data from multiple data sources (ASCII and OLE-DB are the most common types).
- Map incoming data to tables and columns in your data warehouse.
- Transform incoming data into various string types and formats. (For example, a standardized test data file might record a student's name as one field called Student Name, while the data warehouse may require Student First Name, Student Middle Name, and Student Last Name. The ETL tool should be able to split the data in "Student Name" so that it loads properly into the warehouse.)
- Validate incoming data according to predefined business rules.
- Resolve duplicate IDs, names, and other identifiers by applying "fuzzy" logic (e.g., the record for Mark G. Jones is like M. G. Jones and M. Greg Jones. All three records share the same birth date. Is it the same person?).
- Execute custom structured query language (SQL) scripts.
- Store the incoming data in a temporary database before loading any data into the warehouse and allow you to recover from unintended changes.
- Merge database tables and match columns in the data source with column names in the data destination automatically.
- Load data into the warehouse.
- You might also want to consider a data management solution that is "SIF compliant." This certification from the Schools Interoperability Framework (SIF) verifies that a software program will be able to properly share information with software programs from other companies. For additional information see www.sifinfo.org.

An ETL tool might provide additional functions, but these are the basic features that every tool ought to include.

What about the level of expertise typically required for someone to manage an ETL tool? Most fundamental, someone who manages the ETL tool must know your data. Beyond that, knowledge of database terms and relational database management systems such as Oracle or Microsoft SQL Server is required. A grasp of SQL is pretty much indispensable. If you don't know these things, you could learn them in several technical courses, but you may be safer putting a database administrator on the task—either your own or through a service.

A Caution about GIGO

This fundamental rule of technology—garbage in/garbage out—not only remains in effect, it is a key concept when it comes to the usefulness of your data.

One of the most important steps when inputting data is to analyze the data for inaccuracies. Check your data for completeness and accuracy. Be sure that you have clean data or clean the data before you try to use them.

If your data are like ours, and everyone else's we know, they have mistakes and they have gaps. The mistakes are caused by a variety of reasons—keying errors, unexplained glitches. The gaps are just that—holes. Some are even black holes. Sometimes clerks skip boxes when they enter information. They might not have access to the information; they might be rushed; they might not know that you require a blank to be completed. To solve the problem, you may decide to standardize some of your procedures and monitor them more closely. It helps if the people doing the data entry understand the importance of the data and the uses you will make of it. A representative for the data entry clerks may wish to serve on your data-analysis team.

For example, when you input free/reduced-cost lunch information, you probably have only three categories: free, reduced, and paid. Include the category "unknown," so that inaccuracies can be found. Take the list of unknown-status students and determine their status. Then reenter the information in the correct category.

You may think such a potentially tedious process is not worth your time and trouble. Think again. During our first input process we found a large group of students in the "unknown" category rather than in one of the correct categories.

In checking our report, we discovered that these students were largely free-lunch status and that accurate reporting would have brought additional money to the district from the federal lunch program. In addition, the percentage of free-lunch students was higher than had been recorded, thus affecting our attractiveness as a potential grant recipient. Not to mention the fact that we had students who qualified to have a free lunch who were not eating each day.

As you move toward maintaining your information system, ensuring that all who maintain data are doing so accurately is a key to the success of your project. It is essential that you have a system to verify the accuracy of data before it is entered into the warehouse. Once data elements are in the warehouse, you must be able to count on their accuracy. If you've filled your warehouse with garbage, you'll get exactly the same thing out.

If you have systems to be sure your data are accurate before they go into your warehouse, you won't have to worry about the integrity of that data when they are used in a report.

A Tool to Store Data

Once you have the data you plan to use to answer your questions, then someone must put them into one place so you will be able to analyze them. To have your data in the same place, you'll need some sort of digital storage facility (a data warehouse). A data warehouse is your tool to store data. A data warehouse takes the digital data you have loaded with your input tool and stores them so that you can retrieve and analyze the information.

You may choose to keep your data in a warehouse in your district or contract with a technology company to host your warehouse on a remote, secure site. If you choose to maintain the warehouse in your district, be sure that you have technology staff who have the time and experience to devote to the project. Of the pieces we have discussed thus far, the storage tool will be the most static. Someone will need to use the other tools on a regular basis to keep your warehouse up to date.

A Tool to Analyze Data

Individual data elements—whether they are in a spreadsheet or in a data warehouse—give us very little useful information. They are a bit like pieces of a jigsaw puzzle. You must have each piece to complete the puzzle, but the pieces mixed together in the box don't give you a meaningful picture. Data analysis allows us to put these pieces together to make a picture that has meaning.

A tool that analyzes data allows you to generate the information you need to make decisions efficiently. Large amounts of data will envelope you like a blanket of fog if you don't have a plan to deal with it. A computer and a data analyzer enable you to query data, comparing one data element with other data elements. By querying data, you turn data into information that you will then be able to use to make decisions.

The best data-analysis tool is one that lets you aggregate and disaggregate data instantly as you explore your various data elements. You determine that your third-grade students are doing well in science but poorly in math by looking at the mean of their test scores. You wonder if that average applies to all of the subgroups in grade 3 or whether there are noticeable differences among the subgroups. A good data-analysis tool should allow you to drill down through your demographic data to discern patterns without having to reload or recalculate data elements.

A Tool to Report Information

A tool that creates easy-to-understand charts, graphs, and reports allows information to be clearly understood and communicated with various audiences.

The type of report you generate depends on two main factors: (a) the decision you are informing, and (b) the people who are making the decision.

To put that another way:

- What is the question you're asking? Think of the question and report the information in the best way so that it helps you answer your question.
- Who will be answering the question? Think of the decision-making group and report the information in the best way so that the decision makers clearly understand the information and can use it to inform their decision.

It helps if your tool can generate a variety of report formats that enable you to easily develop the reports you need for decision-making and communicating to decision makers. The area of reporting information is the focus of chapter 7.

The relationships among the tool that inputs, the tool that stores, the tool that analyzes, and the tool that reports are critical to your ability to use your system—and maintain your wits while you do so. A key to making the system work is to have software and hardware that enable the input, storing, analysis, and reporting to be done efficiently and easily.

PEOPLE MAKE IT WORK

Do you have the right people on the bus? (Collins 2001)

You can have the hardware and software, but in reality, the people are the ones who really make it work. It's important to have a "mother" or "father" for the project. One person must be responsible for making the data-analysis system happen. The project manager can have others to help, but this is one project that really needs a parent. Most districts find that a person who is well-versed in curriculum, instruction, and assessment is the perfect parent. The parent's responsibility is to coordinate, to continually ask questions, and to keep the data-analysis plan in front of others, helping them see the value that data analysis brings to their campus or program.

Most principals and program directors wear so many hats that finding the time to analyze data seems impossible. The project manager can help other educators see the value through the beginning stages of data analysis so that eventually they begin to find the time to analyze data themselves. Early on, the project manager may find himself asking questions, running reports and taking them to principals and program managers, saying, "What do you think about this?" That's why a parent is needed.

A technical expert is needed to be responsible for the technical side of the project. We discussed the requirements for someone who can input data. That person is usually a very different sort from the project parent.

The technical expert handles the data warehouse, the data input, the data cleansing—in short, the technical data functions. This leaves the parent free to report information in ways that helps others make decisions.

In your data-analysis system, each step flows into the others, leading to a seamless whole that gives you the information you need to answer questions. The process works like this:

1. Determine the question you want to answer based on your goal.
2. Determine the data to collect to answer the question.
3. Collect the data to answer the question.
4. Verify the data.
5. Organize the data.
6. Input the data into the data-analysis system.
7. Set up the query.
8. Run the query against the stored electronic (digital) data.
9. Set up the report format.

10. Generate the desired report.
11. Study the information presented in the report.
12. Use the information to answer the question you asked.
13. Make the data-analysis system a key component of your decision-making process.

Once you develop your data-analysis system the process can be simplified. Each time you ask a new question, if the data are in your system to answer the question, then you are able to move directly from step 1 to step 7, from the question to the query. The power of having a data-analysis system that is maintained regularly begins to show when you are able to inform decisions regularly and routinely because you can go from the question to the query, without the time-consuming steps of collecting, organizing, verifying, and inputting data between these two steps.

Part 2

MOVING FROM DATA TO INFORMATION

Information is what you need to make decisions. Now let's think about how you can begin to turn these mountains of data into information!

In part 1 you started with your goals, asked questions about your goals, and then collected data that would help you answer the questions you asked. You developed your master data directory, with the data sources that you have in your district. If you are interested in getting a data-analysis system, read chapter 5, which has information to think about in selecting a system.

Your journey is off to a good start. At this point you have data and you have analyzed it. Now comes the next curve—information, not just data, is what you need to make decisions.

In part 2 you will turn your mountains of data into information! You'll develop reports that make your information clear to the decision makers, and you'll also find other uses for the information you've worked so hard to produce.

6

Reporting Information

Realtors use the term *curb appeal*, referring to the first impression that clients have as they approach and drive by the property. In the same sense, if a school portfolio isn't visually appealing, the task of engaging people in discussion of the data and its implications for planning and decision-making will be that much more difficult. (Holcomb 1999, 50)

WHY DO YOU REPORT INFORMATION?

Everything you've done with this handbook thus far has been the prelude to this moment. All the question asking and the data gathering have been for one purpose: to turn your data into information. Information, not data, is what you need to make decisions. You have examined your goals, asked your questions, analyzed your data, and are ready to develop a report. Now you have information.

When you develop a report, you have information. You no longer just have data. The main reason you have turned your data into information is so that you can use that information to make decisions. So the first thing you want to think about in reporting your information is, How can you best present this information so that it gives you the clearest picture to help you make the best decision you can make?

To get the clearest picture you can, think about the following aspects of the presentation of the information:
- How do you report information?
- What technical qualities should you consider?
- What do you do with your information after you've used it to make a decision?

We will consider each of these aspects of reporting information in this chapter.

Clarity and excellence in thinking is very much like clarity and excellence in the display of data. When principles of design replicate principles of thought, the act of arranging information becomes an act of insight. (Tufte 1997)

HOW DO YOU REPORT INFORMATION?

To make your information useful, the first step is to put it into a format that makes it readily accessible to the audience. In this case, the audience is the group that is going to use the information to make decisions. The decision may be to fund a program, abandon a staff development initiative, or support a levy for building funds. Even if the group is small, or even if you think the decision is insignificant, take the time to consider the presentation of the report and put the information in a form that enhances the group's ability to use it effectively. In the long run, you'll be glad you made the effort.

The well-designed presentation of interesting data:

• is a matter of substance, of statistics, and of design.
• consists of complete ideas communicated with clarity, precision, and efficiency.
• gives to the viewer the greatest number of ideas in the shortest time with the least ink in the smallest space.
• requires telling the truth about the data (Tufte 1997).

From a purely practical standpoint, your first decision will be whether to use a narrative, a chart, a graph, or some combination of those. If you use a narrative, then your numerical data are embedded in the paragraphs or sentences of information. If you use a combination, then you have some narrative information, along with some graphical representation of the data. Or you can use graphs or charts alone.

If you use charts or graphs, make sure you include a title, labels within the table or figure, or a footnote. Also, your chart or graph should clearly explain who or what is represented, the unit of measurement you used (e.g., percent down, percent across, value, change over time), the time period covered, and the data source. This final, important element helps the audience understand whether your display is based on objective or subjective information (Levesque, Bradby, Rossi, and Teitelbaum 1998).

If you use graphs, and many data-analysis software packages make their use extremely easy, the first thing you need to decide is which type of graph to use. Information can look very different depending on which type of graph or chart you use, or by how you line up the same chart in different ways.

Common Forms of Graphs

There are a number of graphs from which to choose. The most common include the following:

- bar graph
- histogram
- line graph
- pie chart
- scatter plot

Bar graphs (see chart 6.1) are probably the most common type of graph used to display data in education. They are also usually the "default" graph in most off-the-shelf graphing software. Just because they are easy and available, though, doesn't mean they are always the appropriate choice.

The best use of bar graphs is to make visual comparisons when there is a strong trend in your data (our test scores are going up!) or a strong difference between groups of variables (girls outscored boys 2:1 on the science end-of-course assessment!). Be careful not to add too much information to your bar chart; don't try to show more than 10 variables. In fact, you'd be better off to limit yourself to four to six.

A histogram (see chart 6.2) looks a lot like a bar chart (and we've heard them mistaken one for the other), but the difference is that you use a histogram to plot continuous data so the bars touch.

Chart 6.1. Bar Graph

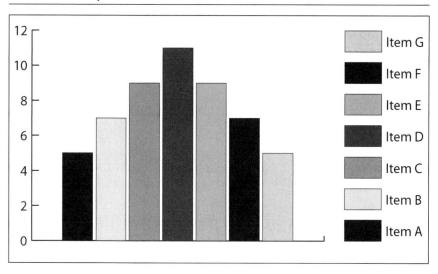

Chart 6.2. Histogram

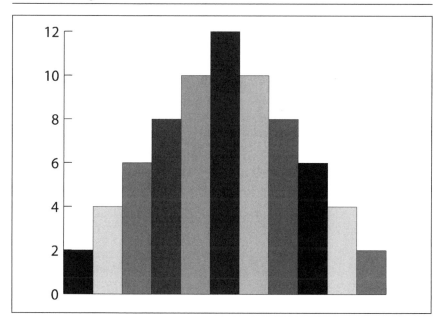

Consider the following example: Take an informal survey of the teachers in your school and ask them how many and what kind of pets they have. You might be able to show their responses in a bar chart that looks like chart 6.3.

Chart 6.3. Bar Graph—Pets

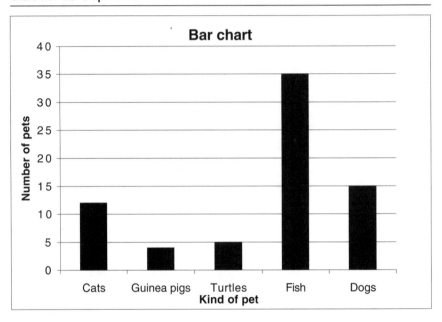

Chart 6.4. Histogram—Pets

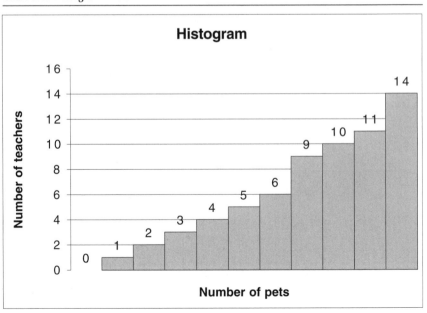

Whether the pets are dogs, cats, fish, turtles or guinea pigs, each group is distinct and represented by a separate bar on the chart. No teachers share their pets, so there is no continuous data to plot. On the other hand, if you were to chart the total number of pets you would have continuous data and use a histogram (see chart 6.4). In that case you could arrange your bars in ascending order and have a range, or continuum from 0 to 14. Of course, you could also arrange the data in descending order, with the range from 14 to 0.

Line graphs (see chart 6.5) always represent data collected over time. They are useful when you want to display information collected over several years or when you want to track trends. You should not display more than three to five sets of information and all of the sets should be complete for all of the years in your graph.

Chart 6.5. Line Graph

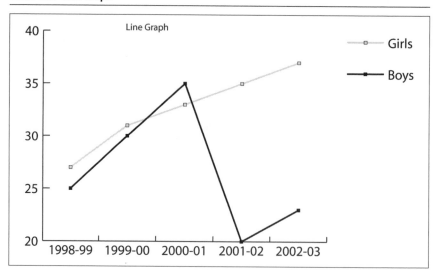

Pie charts (see chart 6.6) are most appropriate to show the parts of a whole relationship where the total percent is 100. For example, you might use a pie chart to show percentages of students by ethnic groups. As with

Chart 6.6. Pie Chart

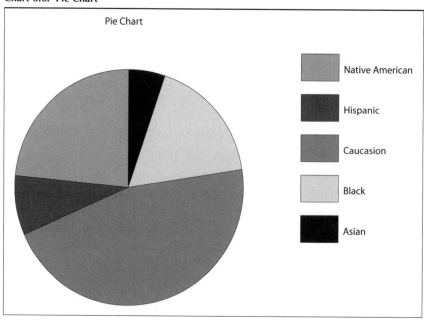

line and bar graphs, you should not use pie charts to show more than five to eight segments. If you have two pie charts side by side, be sure to place the comparable elements in the same relative wedges of the pies. Exploded pie charts, especially the ones that have all the wedges exploded, should not even be in your graphing toolbox.

Kosslyn (1994) does a much better job of explaining when to use a scatter plot (see chart 6.7) than we could. He says we should:

- use a scatter plot to convey an overall impression of the relation between two variables.
- convey the overall trend, not individual values.
- not include a grid on our scatter plot.
- avoid illustrating more than one independent variable in a scatter plot.
- fit a line through a scatter plot to show how closely two variables are related. (pp. 154–58)

Chart 6.7. Scatter Plot

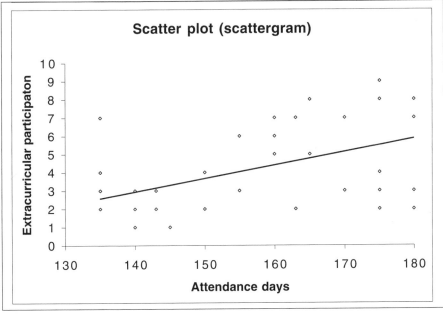

How many dimensions do you really need?

Almost every chart type comes in a 3-D version. These 3-D versions are pretty to look at, but if you use them too often you may find that you've sacrificed substance for form. Attempting to show a three-dimensional display with a two-dimensional media (like a computer screen or sheet of paper) can result in incorrect inferences regarding what the chart portrays. We won't go so far as to say that you should totally avoid 3-D charts, but we do ask that you use your power for good (unlike what we did in chart 6.8). Rarely is there a time when a 3-D chart is useful in presenting educational information.

Chart 6.8. 3-D Chart

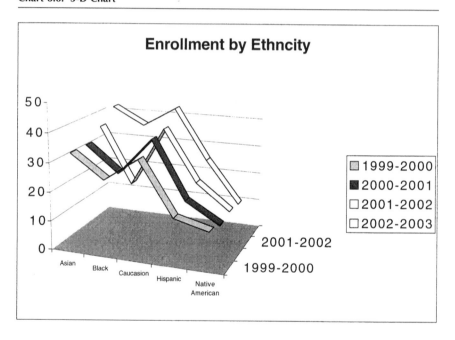

WHAT TECHNICAL QUALITIES SHOULD YOU CONSIDER?

As you construct the presentation of your information, consider the following technical qualities: (a) size, (b) introduction, (c) legend, (d) labeling graphs, and (e) use of color.

Size

Consider the size of your report. The size is based on the needs of the audience. If you are using an overhead projector or PowerPoint, either be sure the print is large enough so that everyone—even the people in the back of the room with over-40 eyes—can see and read the print; or give them a hard copy of the information and use the projected slide for a visual reference.

Many schools and districts keep an 8½-by-11-inch notebook with all their reports, one per page, with a master copy and a transparency of each one. That way, whenever a report is needed, copies can be made for use, and the transparency can be used and returned to the notebook. You might also consider keeping a disk or CD of your slides in the front pocket of the notebook so you can reproduce quantities of originals without having to remember just where you stored them on your hard drive.

If the report is going to be bound in a book, remember to account for space for margins and for the binding. Usually you should allow one and a half inches on the side of the page that is to be bound or hole punched for inclusion in a notebook. Also, consider including each of the following components in your report.

Introduction

This can be a short paragraph with a basic explanation of what the display represents. Even if a small, informal group is using the information, including an introduction will keep you from having to explain over and over what the information is about. It also gives you a complete record for your data notebook. For example, if you're reporting on test results, include the name of the test and when it was given, as well as which and how many students. If you anticipate that your audience may not know much about the test, you might want to include a few sentences explaining the type of test and the reason your district administered it.

Legend

A legend is an explanatory list of symbols in a graph. If you use more than one data set, you need to include a legend. Avoid using acronyms and abbreviations that may be clear to you but not to others who may be using the graph. For example, you may understand "F/RL" but your audience

may not be aware that you're trying to explain something about students
who receive Free or Reduced Price Lunches.

Labeling Graphs

When labeling graphs, there are a few guidelines to follow:

- *Label each axis clearly.* Again, you should avoid those abbreviations
  and acronyms. Also steer clear of fancy typefaces. A graph illustrating the success of the reading program you want to convince the
  school board to refund is not the place to show off your facility with
  the variations of Bodoni fonts. Use a familiar serif font with an appropriate mixture of capital and lowercase letters.
- *Label your values correctly.* If you use percentile scores do not use
  the % sign; show percentile scores as the number with the word percentile along the side, or add the "ile" suffix to the number (15%ile),
  or print the number (52nd, 33rd).
- *Be accurate and consistent with your choice of ranges.* Usually the
  range is shown on the vertical axis. It's best to show the entire range.
  Otherwise, scores may appear higher than they actually are. For example, on a test you are reporting, the range of possible scores is
  0–100. The actual scores fall between 72 and 100. You may be
  tempted to set your vertical axis with a range from 50–100 rather than
  0–100. If you do, the scores will look different visually (which is to
  say, higher) on the 50–100 scale than they do on the 0–100 scale. In
  addition to the problem of visually inflating scores by changing the
  vertical axis, if you are showing a number of reports and change the
  vertical axis on various charts, the audience may become confused
  about the data. For these reasons, a scale showing the entire range is
  generally the best way to represent the information on a chart.

Use of Color

- *Use color and patterns to clearly distinguish your data set.* Be careful using color. Use basic colors with good contrast. Remember the
  cost of color copies. Your graphs need to make sense when repro-

duced in black and white. Also consider using the same color for the same data element in a series of graphs that you will present together (e.g., white males are always represented by a red bar). Don't make your readers work too hard to get information from your graph. They might not consider it worth the effort.

Also be careful of patterns. What looks great on your computer screen might be totally weird when printed or seen from the back of the room. Using a different pattern for each section of bar graphs and pie graphs and a different type of line for a line graph, along with making each section or line different colors, will let you see the distinctions when you make black-and-white copies.

We suggest that you make a black-and-white copy of every color graph you plan to use so that you can check it for clarity. That way, if you ever need a black-and-white version, you know it will make sense. One final note on color: if you plan to show your graph to 100 men, count on at least seven of them being color deficient or color-blind (the percent is much lower for women). They may have difficulty distinguishing the red bar on your graph from the green one. If you simply must have color, consider using blue, which can be distinguished by most color-deficient viewers.

> **It is easy to be dazzled by a display of data, especially if it is rendered with color or depth. . . . The success of a visualization tool should be based solely on the amount we learn about the phenomenon under study. (Cleveland 1993, 1)**

The way you plan to use your information, along with the target audience, will influence the format in which you present your information. Even if your data-analysis software produces graphs and tables for you, the most appropriate formats to use may take some thought on your part. While highlighting your data and pressing your F11 key may create a perfectly serviceable graph in a popular database software, you will probably have to make a few adjustments to allow your graph to tell the story you're hoping to convey.

We want you to create pleasing charts that deliver a wealth of information to your viewers. We want you to avoid what Rand (1993) calls the "Triumph of decoration over information." But we need to be very, very clear about something here. We are not suggesting that you should use bright colors, innovative graphing styles, creative labeling, or other devices to obscure, or be less than truthful about, your data. Data are data are data. You are seeking information and you must not compromise your quest.

Once you have developed your report, look at it and ask yourself, Does your report:

- focus on the question you asked?
- show the content of the information?
- make large data sets understandable?
- encourage comparisons of data?
- present coherent visual and written messages?
- present information clearly?

If so, then you are ready for a final check. Ask someone in your school who hasn't seen your report to look at it and explain it to you. If they can do that, then you should be ready to meet with your group to consider the information.

It is a psychological, not a moral, fact that people do not like to expend effort and often will not bother to do so, particularly if they are not sure in advance that the effort will be rewarded. (Kosslyn 1994, 10)

Now that you have transformed your data into information to serve as the basis for your decision-making, you will have many questions to ask about the information in the report. We've gone into detail about questions you might consider in chapter 7, The Search for Leverage Points.

We'd also like for you to consider what other uses you can make of the report and why. We've gone into detail about uses and reasons to use reports of information in chapter 8, What Do You Do with Your Report after You've Used It for Decision-Making?

7

The Search for Leverage Points

Data help us answer the primary question "What do we do next?" amid the panoply of competing opportunities for action. (Schmoker 1996, 42)

WHAT WILL YOU DO WITH YOUR INFORMATION FIRST?

You had an important question to answer. That is why you wanted to analyze data and turn it into information to inform your decision. What is the answer to your question? How will that answer inform your decision? Most important, *what will you do differently as a result of knowing the answer to your question?* The first thing we suggest is that your team write down the answers to those questions.

You can also expand your answers into formal summary statements about your information. What does your information mean? What did you learn from studying it? What will you do as a result of studying the information?

You can summarize the report in a variety of ways. Several are listed here.

- State how the report relates to the goals of the school or district. This type of summary is especially valuable since your report is based on a question about one of your goals.

- List statements of strengths and areas of concern about the information presented on the report.
- State the actions you will take as a result of the information on the report.

You might have several reports that relate to one another, with one summary statement for all of them.

NOW WHAT?

Often what happens is that your group answers the original question and finds that the answer brings up many new questions. Many times this leads to a search for leverage points. While answering your original question is vitally important, moving beyond the answer to one question to the search for leverage points can be extremely exciting and valuable to the school or district.

Leverage points are the places where you can impact the system with a relatively small amount of pressure and a great amount of gain. Finding leverage points and using them to create positive change become the big payoffs in an information-based decision-making system. Leverage points are the pot of gold at the end of the rainbow.

How do you find leverage points? Think in terms of creating focus, finding problems, identifying alternative solutions to those problems, and targeting your resources more efficiently.

In the search for leverage points, we like to begin with the short list of questions that Schmoker (1996, 42) poses:

- What are data telling us?
- What problems or challenges do they reveal?
- What can we do about what data reveal?
- What strategies should we brainstorm?
- What research should we consult?
- What are data telling us about how effective our current efforts are in helping achieve our goals?
- What do we do next?

You can ask a lot of good questions once you have a report with information, not just isolated data elements. Asking each of Schmoker's questions regarding your report is a great place to start in the search for leverage points.

Using information for leverage is the big payoff. Without clear indications that change needs to happen, most people and systems are content to keep doing what they were doing before. It's hard to break the cycle of inertia. If you stop to think about it, that's really pretty logical. We are no longer a nomadic society. Our food now comes to us; we don't have to go to the food. We don't have to move around to survive. Change, however, takes energy, resources, and commitment. All of us, personally and organizationally, have limited energy, resources, and commitment. So without clear and compelling reasons to change, we continue doing what we are doing. Data, when presented to people informatively, can help them see what needs to be changed. Once people see what needs to be changed, they can then begin to develop the internal will to change it. Leverage implies both of these aspects—seeing the need for change and having the will to commit to the change. Data, when used masterfully, provide just the tool to give people a clear picture of why this change needs to happen at this time.

Mr. Martinez joined the fourth-grade team at Abraham Lincoln Elementary School in the fall. When he was interviewed by the principal and teacher team, he learned that the district and school were committed to the concept of "working on the work," providing engaging work for students so that the students would learn the important concepts they needed to learn, as advocated by Phillip C. Schlechty (2002). He wasn't sure exactly what that meant, but he viewed himself as a designer of quality work for students and believed that working on a team that thought the same way would be professionally satisfying.

Early in the fall, Mr. Martinez taught a unit on measurement in mathematics that he had taught for several years. He thought the unit was good. Students usually did it without complaining, made good grades on the assignments and test, and it included the state standards. It also had several hands-on activities that were fun for the students to do. This time, in addition, his team designed Student Engagement Measures that they used after each unit. Students indicated how engaged they were in the unit: authentically engaged (I enjoyed the unit, learned a lot by doing it); ritually engaged (I did the unit for the grade or for my teacher); passively compliant (I did the unit because I had to); retreatism (I barely did anything at all); or rebellion (I did nothing and rebelled against it).

Mr. Martinez was absolutely sure that most of the students were authentically engaged, with some ritual engagement. When he tallied their papers, he was shocked. Students reported that they were mostly passively compliant, with some ritual engagement (15 passively compliant; 7 ritually engaged). He shook his head and said to the team, "Well, you said that we don't know the level of their engagement till we ask them. This really proves it to me. Now I need to do two things. I need you to help me think about the changes I need to make in this unit for next year. But, more important, I need you to help me think about the changes I need to make in the unit I'm teaching next week."

What other data can Mr. Martinez collect from his students to help him? What data helped him see the need for change? Why were these data powerful? What situations have you experienced where data clarified the need for change? What situations have you experienced where data use could have clarified the need for change, but didn't?

Many times it is the question behind the first question (or behind the sixth or seventh question) that will bring the big "aha." Just as you can drill down in data, you can drill down in questions. What may seem obvious isn't always the case. After you ask a question, ask "Why?" then ask "Why?" again and again, until you simply don't have any more questions. This helps keep you from accepting surface answers to difficult problems—leverage points won't be found with surface answers.

QUESTIONS TO FIND LEVERAGE POINTS

We've already given you Schmoker's questions. Here are some more questions that may cause you to think about your information in different ways. Asking yourself relevant questions will help you find your leverage points.

Questions Anyone Might Ask
- What important points jump out at me when I look at the report?
- What questions can I ask about the information in the report?
- What can I learn as a result of examining the report?
- What new questions arise from examining the report?

- How can I use the information in the report to identify successful strategies for teaching targeted groups of students?
- What patterns/trends do I see from examining the report?
- What similarities do I see among information on different reports?
- What differences do I see among information on different reports?
- What do I see in the information that surprises me?
- What do I see that I expected?
- In what other ways can I view the information?
- What other questions can I ask about this information?
- What other reports can I generate that will answer questions that I'm now asking?
- What conclusions can I make about the information?
- What connections do I see between information on different reports?
- How does this information compare with what I expected to find?
- How does the information compare with our goals?
- How does the information compare with current research/literature on the topic?
- How does this information inform our future actions?
- What does this information mean in terms of current student performance and behavior? Preferred student performance and behavior?
- What needs for school improvement might arise from this information?
- How might other stakeholders benefit from this information?
- What good news is there to celebrate?

Questions Teachers Might Ask

- Are there differences among student groups shown in the report?
- Does the report suggest that specific professional development is needed?
- Does the report suggest that specific teaching strategies are working?
- Where do our students need help?
- What concepts do our students understand? What concepts are they failing to understand?
- What are we seeing at the student level? Classroom level? Grade level?
- What are the implications for our curriculum and instructional practices?
- What does the information tell us about the current conditions of the students? Classrooms? Grade level?

Questions Principals Might Ask
- Are students achieving the desired results?
- Are some groups of students achieving at different levels than other groups of students?
- What kinds of professional development would help teachers improve instructional practice?
- Does this report suggest ways the campus might expend its resources to support instruction?
- Is there a difference in what I am seeing at the classroom level? Grade level? School level?
- What are the implications for curriculum and instructional practice on this campus?
- What does the information tell us about the current conditions of the students? Classrooms? Grade levels?

Questions Program Managers Might Ask
- What am I seeing at the grade level? School level? Program level? District level?

- What are the implications for curriculum and instructional practices?
- What does the information tell us about the current conditions of the student groups? Programs? Schools? District?
- What levels of student learning are our current programs producing?

Questions Superintendents and Boards of Trustees Might Ask

- What changes does this report suggest need to be made in current programs to produce desired results?
- Which schools need more assistance? What kind of assistance?
- Which programs need to be piloted? Expanded? Abandoned?

SUMMARIZE YOUR CONCLUSIONS

You and your team have asked lots of questions about the information in the report. It's time to summarize your conclusions. Take the questions that were relevant to your report and write these questions and your answers. Put them with your report and the original summary. Now, you have an information-based decision-making road map.

This road map gives you a record of where you are right now in the use of this report. This record establishes the value of this information to you and your team. It will help you decide where you need to go next. In short, it becomes a part of your road map.

8

What Do You Do with Your Report after You've Used It for Decision-Making?

> Information is power because it gives us the best alternative to the crystal ball for making predictions that can ultimately prevent future failure and ensure future successes. (Bernhardt 2000, 66)

After you have used your report for decision-making and have searched for leverage points, you have two choices. You may either retire the report to the archives or you may introduce it to a broader audience for a different purpose. In this chapter we'll suggest possible purposes and audiences who might benefit from your reported information.

WHAT ARE YOUR PURPOSES FOR REPORTING INFORMATION?

This would seem such an obvious question that some of you are wondering why we've asked it. But, while some of the answers are very obvious, other answers aren't quite as obvious as you might think.

Reporting for Decision-Making

Reporting information helps us to look for patterns within the data to inform our decisions. Thinking through the data together allows us to use our collective brainpower to recognize relationships and trends among the data. Patterns, relationships, and trends are important because they help us avoid knee-jerk reactions to one-time events and help us take a longer-term view to solving problems.

Some people are tempted to tamper. Tampering is adjusting the system without knowing the effect those adjustments will have on the system. Every adjustment will have consequences. If you don't think about the consequences, those consequences will become "unintended consequences." Even with the best planning and thought, you'll find a few unintended consequences, but with tampering you'll always get problems.

Of course, the very worst sort of tampering is to make a huge change to a system based solely on rumor or perceptions. We know that if you even opened this book, you know better than to tamper that way. The second-worst kind of tampering is caused by making a huge change to the system based on a single bit of data. One way to avoid tampering is to make decisions based on patterns in the data. It is important to always look for patterns in data and make changes based on patterns, not on a single, isolated data point. Victoria Bernhardt (2000a) talks about the concept of "triangulation," using at least three data points to make decisions. Decisions based on patterns of data, not just single points, help you avoid tampering.

Sunny Side High School was proud of its high school program— and of its students' SAT scores. Sunny Side students' average SAT scores were consistently higher than 1100. Students were regularly admitted to the colleges and universities of their choice. The district had a strong pre-AP and AP curriculum, an SAT prep class that students could register for if they wished, and tutoring available after school as needed. The high school also had a strong extracurricular program, including athletics, band, drama, and choir. Students in these activities practiced after school.

Mrs. Yee, the high school principal, sat at her desk with her head in her hands, however, because her world had just fallen apart. This year's SAT scores had just came in and the average score was less than 950. This had never happened before. The community was sure to make an enormous outcry. What should she do? Her first thought was to meet with her campus leadership team.

The team was as flabbergasted as she was. They had to develop a plan. Here's their plan:

• Make SAT prep a requirement for all students.
• Make tutoring a requirement for all students after school.
• Revamp the pre-AP/AP curriculum.

Is this team tampering? Why or why not? What could some unintended consequences be of the proposals the team is considering? Are such program changes needed based on one data point? What if the team disaggregated the data to look for a pattern within this SAT data to better understand it? Are there other data they could consider to help them search for a pattern? What if the team had a data-analysis tool that would help them verify the accuracy of the reported results? Are there other situations where you have seen schools make decisions based on single data points? What unintended consequences of those decisions have you witnessed? What procedures do you put in place to avoid unintended consequences of decisions?

Reporting information helps us determine whether our assumptions about the situation are correct or incorrect. Putting the data together, analyzing it, and seeing it on paper can help us affirm or dispel what we think is true. For years we made decisions in education by hunches; many times that was all we had. We don't have to—and we can't afford to—do that anymore. Data help us decide whether our hunches and educated guesses are right or wrong.

Information gives feedback—should we keep going the way we are going, make minor adjustments, or make a complete change? Without feedback we don't know.

Feedback gives a reason to expand, abandon, or improve programs, allowing us to keep the focus on learning results by measuring program effectiveness. We are historically hesitant to abandon anything we have started. Information can give us the basis for making the decisions to abandon programs that have not met their goals, have outlasted their effectiveness, or are not cost-effective.

We report information so that we can identify groups of students who are improving and groups who are not, and so that we can determine why this is happening and what to do about it.

We report information so that we raise questions. Many times we raise more questions than we answer. This is a very good thing. Having more questions than answers causes us to examine more deeply what we are doing with programs, with children, and with decisions and enables us to be more deliberate with our actions.

> **I find that a great part of the information I have was acquired by looking up something and finding something else on the way. (Franklin P. Adams, 1881–1960)**

We report information because it helps us get to the root causes of problems so we don't waste time and energy on superficial solutions. Information makes the invisible visible. Not only do we get to the root causes of problems, we also find problems surface that might never otherwise be seen, because we are analyzing data and looking at what we find. Often finding the problem is much harder than finding the solution.

Reporting information allows us to target resources to our leverage points for improvement, getting the biggest bang for our buck. Information also provides the basis for our school/district improvement plans and processes, helping us determine whether we are accomplishing what we set out to accomplish.

Reporting to Tell Your Story

Your main purpose for reporting information is often so you can use the information to make decisions. There are other important reasons to report information to other audiences. One is telling your story to the audience.

The power of telling your story is incredible. People remember concepts through stories that make the concepts clear. You can use your report as the basis of your story, wrap your story around the report, and communicate so that what you say is remembered and internalized by the audience. When that happens, others are able to appreciate and possibly replicate your success.

> You've no doubt heard the story of a little girl who was watching her mom prepare to bake a ham. Just before her mother placed the ham in the baking pan, the girl noticed that she cut off a small section from both ends of the ham.
>
> "Why do you do that, Mommy?" asked the girl.
>
> Her mom answered, "I don't know. That's how my mother did it. Let's ask her." So they called Grandmother and inquired about her method of baking a ham. "Why do you cut a piece of meat from each end of the ham before putting it in the baking pan?" the little girl asked.
>
> "Well, let me think a minute," her grandmother answered. "You know, I can't remember. All I know is that's the way my mother always did it."
>
> It so happened that the little girl's great-grandmother was still living. So the next time they were together, the girl said, "Great-grandmother, why is it that you cut one small piece of meat from each end of the ham before you baked it?" After thinking about it for a long moment, the ninety-year-old great-grandmother answered, "Oh, I remember now. I cut the ends off of the ham because my baking pan was too small."
>
> Using such a story is much more effective than simply saying, "We need to quit doing things without checking to see if they are right for us." (Plunkett, 2002)

Reporting to Gain Community Support

We report information because it helps us clearly show the reality of our schools to the community, providing the community with meaningful information on our performance and any other information of community interest. Reports to parents and the community might include question-and-answer letters, brochures explaining ways that they might interpret the scores found in the reports, and posting on the district's website.

You should also remember the possibility that not everyone in your community will be able to read the same language. Your reports to gain community support should be written so that your entire community will have the opportunity to read and understand them.

Reporting to Gain Support for Continuous Improvement

Reporting information gains internal and external support for change and continuous improvement, helping us to continue things that are working and stop things that aren't working. As our internal and external publics see our progress through our documentation, then we have additional opportunities to make more progress and we fuel the cycle of continuous improvement.

Who Are Your Possible Audiences?

As you think about the purposes for communicating the information in your report, you may want to consider the potential audiences for that communication. Of course, the audience and method of communication you select depend on the purpose or purposes of your sharing the information with them.

The audiences who might benefit from having an opportunity to see your report include the following:

- administrators
- boards of trustees
- civic organizations
- district or school accountability committee
- legislators
- local officials (county council, city council)
- parents/community via meetings
- parents/community via special mailings
- parent–teacher organizations
- public via the broadcast media
- public via the print media
- public via school or district report card
- school councils
- social service agencies
- students
- support staff
- teachers

Our purpose here is not to write an exhaustive treatise on reporting, communicating, and public relations. But we do want to give some additional food for thought as you move toward sharing the information you've created.

9

What Do You Do with Your Road Map Now That You Have It?

> We have found that when schools document where they are and where they want to be, their growth and progress will encourage them to continue implementing change and moving forward. Those who do not document lose track of where they are and what they agreed to do. (Bernhardt 2000b, xiv)

At this point you have done a tremendous amount of work. You and your team have collected, decided, pondered, considered, discussed—maybe argued a bit—and now you have your road map.

Stop a minute, take a deep breath, and congratulate yourself. You've followed the road and developed a road map that you and others can use from now on, but only if you refine it as the road changes.

Remember the last road map you used on a long family vacation? No doubt it was in more than one piece by the end of the trip. By the end of our last road trip, our atlas was missing a few key states. Texas had fallen out and was lost somewhere along the way, along with parts of Oklahoma and Louisiana. There was a dead bug between the pages of California and a large drop of dried fudge ice cream obscuring Omaha.

The same thing, or hopefully just similar things, will happen to you if you don't have a plan for keeping your road map together. So, if you haven't already done so, stop now and put the entire document into one place.

That place might be electronic storage, it might be a hard copy, or it might be both. One of us went to a friend's mother's funeral with a copy of her dissertation on a disk in her coat pocket. There are some things in which you've just invested too much time to want to take chances.

You may want each person to have a notebook. You might decide to put it all in a file cabinet. You might decide to do all those things. You make the decision. The point of your doing all this hard work was so that you would have a road map to follow. If you lose the road map, your work has been wasted.

Earlier we suggested that you compile a data notebook, or folder on your computer, to record the process you used to develop your road map. At this point it includes all the forms you have completed, the notes from every meeting, the decisions you made, and who implemented each decision. You dated each document and listed the people present at the meeting, along with those who completed the information on each form. You have kept a clear written record of your project so far.

You also have a master data directory. It includes your data sources based on the data formats, locations, and people or departments who have data. The directory serves as your document to organize data collection, allowing your process to achieve efficiency and avoid duplication of effort.

Now we suggest that you add the third tool—an information-based decision-making road map. This third tool is the place where you keep the actual reports and the summaries of the information you generate and upon which you have made decisions. As with the others, it may be an actual notebook or a file on your computer. But having all your reports together in one place allows you to systematically keep up with the process of using them in your decision-making—and will allow others in the organization to be involved in the process and replicate it.

These three tools, along with the questions you and your team consider next will form the basis of your information master plan. Continued data collection and analysis requires a plan. Your team will want to consider the following questions as it develops an ongoing plan. Otherwise you

may end up with a "one-time" project that was nice but didn't make much of a difference for your school or district.

As you plan your next steps, you might want to consider defining the tasks that will be involved as well as the position that will be responsible for maintaining your data-collection system. Table 9.1 may give you some ideas.

Include your data-collection worksheets with your road map, and it will be your steadfast guide into the future. You might even find that you're ready to answer some of those "nice-to-know" questions now. Here are some questions to start you thinking:

- Which goals do you plan to add?
- What questions do you plan to ask about the goals?
- What data will you collect in the future to answer your questions?
- What questions will you plan to answer using these data?
- How will you collect the data?
- Who will be responsible?
- What will the schedule be for collection of the data?
- What format will the data be in?
- Where will they be stored?
- When will the data be input into your storage system?
- When will they be available for data analysis?
- Who will analyze the data?
- What types of analysis will you do using this data?
- What reports will you generate for information?
- What format will the report be in?
- Who will put it in that format?
- What else will you do with the report?
- Who will the audience be?
- Where will the report be stored?
- When and how will it be updated?

Be sure to conduct ongoing data meetings with your team. We suggest that you plan these meetings on a scheduled basis. The schedule will depend on your use of data and your own needs. Make it a practice to use an agenda format that will serve as a memory jogger and reminder to think about your data collection and analysis, along with your current goals and

Table 9.1.

Type of Problem	Sample Responsibilities Related to Data-Analysis Warehouse
Instructional Leadership (School Board, Superintendent, Associate/Assistant Superintendents)	Require the use of data analysis warehouse queries as basis for instructional and budgetary decisions.
Technology Specialist	Provide means by which data can be entered and verified (e.g., student scheduling software).
Site and Department Administrators	Ensure that student/teacher/class level data is maintained in digital format and entered in a timely manner.
Site and Department Support Staff	Enter data correctly and in a timely manner.
Testing Coordinator	Ensure that test data is available in digital form and delivered to the person responsible for data verification and loading.
Technology Specialist	Verify data prior to loading in warehouse. Load warehouse data at regular intervals.
Technology Specialist/Data Analyst/ Professional Development resource persons	Provide training in the use of warehouse and software as a part of new employee orientation with retraining as appropriate
Technology Specialist/Data Analyst	Serve as liaison with warehouse provider's customer service to channel all inquiries regarding data and queries and to ensure software upgrades are installed as available.
Site or Department Administrators— the users of the warehouse	Run queries as dictated by the needs of the school or district; might include running of periodic or prescheduled reports (e.g., once semiannual test data is loaded) or queries in response to specific requests regarding schools, teachers, programs, or reports needed for accreditation, awards, etc. Assist other users with queries, favorites, etc.
District-Level Instructional Leader	Determine data to be included in warehouse and intervals for loading; periodically reassess usefulness of data being loaded into warehouse in conjunction with users.
Professional Development resource persons	Provide training for users in data interpretation and communication via in-house or contract training.

questions, and future goals and questions—in short, a reminder to keep moving along with your data into the future.

Items you might want to include in your meetings and on your agenda:

- Specify (and slavishly follow) beginning and ending times.
- Establish ground rules for handling discussion and disagreements.
- Review current goals, questions.
- Review data notebook and master data directory.
- Review future goals, questions, data collection.

At this point, you have three major tools to assist you in your information-based decision-making—your data notebook, your master data directory, and your information-based decision-making road map. These tools will help you move on down the road of information-based decision-making.

Part 3

TEST PRIMER

Part 3 gives you a primer on standardized tests in specific information in plain language that helps you know what you can—and cannot—do with test data as you use it to inform your decisions.

Take the goals that you have regarding student achievement and the questions you've asked that involve standardized test data, and turn to chapter 10. There you'll find information that will help you understand those mountains of score reports from the testing companies.

10

Testing, Testing 1, 2, 3

> This life is a test; it is only a test. If it were real life you would re-
> ceive instructions on where to go and what to do. (Anonymous)

We face tests every day. At the broadest level, the act of driving to work
is a "performance assessment" of your ability to translate your knowledge
of traffic laws and driving fundamentals into practice. To cook dinner, you
must use your math skills. To program your VCR, you must prove your
ability to read technical writing and to translate that writing into a manual
sequence, i.e., you have to know which buttons to push.

In schools, we use verbal tests, observations, and teacher-made written
tests daily to monitor student progress and to modify instruction to meet
students' instructional needs.

For the most part, both the assessments and the results are fairly
straightforward.

- Can the student add three-digit numbers?
- Can the student explain the steps involved in making a sugar-water
  solution?
- Can the student write a sonnet?
- Can the student write a critique of a play?

Teachers understand these types of assessments. If a teacher gives a test and most of the students can't add three-digit numbers, then the teacher repeats the lesson. If most students in the class can add three-digit numbers, then the teacher may provide some remedial instruction to the ones who can't and move on to subtraction with the ones who can. The ability to understand the outcomes of those tests and to make those kinds of adjustments is well within the comfort zone of most teachers.

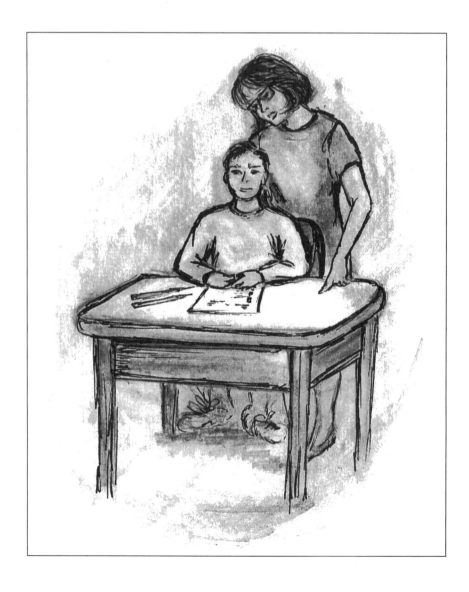

Then, periodically, schools give a different kind of test: the *standardized* test. Teachers prepare students both intellectually and mentally for these very different tests. They give practice tests so the students will be familiar with the test format. They accompany the "administration" of these tests, which are much too important just to "give," with instructions to students to "bring No. 2 pencils," "get a good night's sleep," "eat a good breakfast," "bubble-in your answers completely," "come back to the ones you don't know," "write legibly," "don't make stray marks on your paper," and a multitude of other test-taking tips. All this really does let students know that a *standardized* test is very different from other tests they take in school.

Standardized test scores come back from a testing company on a score report. In reality they come back on many pages of a score report and on a diskette, data tape, or, most likely, a compact disk. For many years, when the scores came back, we gave them to the teachers and said, "Here are your scores from last year's students." Now we give them to the principal and say, "You are accountable for these scores for the students' performance last year." But what do the scores mean?

Hmmm. Could we use a little help here? Unless you have a master's degree of some sort, you've probably never had a college-level course in measurement and statistics. If you have had such a course, chances are you didn't truly understand all the concepts when you were taking the course. Even if you really understood college-level measurement and statistics when you took it, you've probably forgotten what little bit you did learn because you made a pact with your creator that if you could just get out of the course alive, you'd never say π again. If you understood the concepts then, you probably don't see much connection between the course you took in college and your current reality in reading a standardized test score report. If you can identify with any of that, this chapter is for you.

Your current reality is that you have made a commitment to data analysis and you know that part of the data you will be analyzing is standardized test data. You have begun to develop your road map. Understanding a few simple (really!) concepts will help you as you transform your data into usable information for use in decision-making.

Is the information in this chapter a comprehensive look at statistics?

You ask the silliest things! Of course it isn't! Most of us would agree that "user-friendly statistics" is an oxymoron.

Read these chapters anyway. Not only will you feel better about your-self because of your enlightenment, you'll also be able to avoid assuming the "stuffed Teddy Bear look" when someone asks you a question about your data. And you will have confidence that you are manipulating and analyzing test data correctly.

STANDARDIZED TESTS

We'll begin with a test of our own. Choose the best answer from the mul-tiple choices below each question.

Question 1: What are standardized tests?
  A. The tests that generate the most reported data.
  B. Tests that are intended to provide valid, reliable, and unbi-ased information about students' knowledge of various areas.
  C. Tests that are given and scored in a predetermined manner, including the same way (i.e., in a group setting), the same di-rections, same time limits, same scoring criteria.
  D. All of the above.
  Answer: D. All of the above.

The term *standardized* refers to the format for giving the test, not a re-lationship to standards. The real key to the definition of a standardized test is the giving and scoring of the tests. Standardized tests are always given to students at the same time (e.g., fall administration versus spring ad-ministration) and always scored the same way (e.g., using rubrics to score writing samples). A standardized test is accompanied by a test administra-tor's manual that contains all the rules and regulations for administer-ing the test. These rules must be strictly followed, or the test is invalid.

A standardized test can have students respond to many types of ques-tions and use many answer types. Standardized tests are not limited to multiple-choice answers, but may include true/false, short answer or even essay responses.

Some would take issue with whether choice B in question 1 is correct. They would argue that the standardized tests are biased in various ways, and therefore inferences about what students have learned are not valid.

These people may have a point. You might want to read more about that issue. But that's not the purpose of this section of this guidebook. So, please note the "are intended to" part of choice B and let's move on.

APTITUDE AND ACHIEVEMENT TESTS

Question 2: What are the types of standardized tests?
  A. Aptitude tests
  B. Achievement tests
  C. Adagio tests
  D. Anxiety tests
  E. A and B
  Answer. E. Aptitude and Achievement (and yes, there's probably a little Anxiety thrown in).

An aptitude test is a cognitive (knowledge) test that measures students' abilities to learn skills and to succeed at a task, as well as their ability, skill, talent, or readiness to learn. Aptitude tests once were called intelligence tests.

Remember the SAT? It was originally called the Scholastic Aptitude Test and was designed to be a predictable measure of success in the first year of college. Now it is called the Scholastic Assessment Test. The name was changed because the test manufacturer included questions in the newer versions that test components of the high school curriculum. But it is still used as an aptitude test. Also, despite widespread, numerous, and frequent admonitions from the College Board it is still used by some to judge school quality—but that's another tangent we don't need to pursue. If you want to do so on your own, check out books and videos by James Popham listed in the references.

Back to aptitude tests. The original purpose of aptitude tests, when designed for use by the U.S. Army during World War I, was to sort those who took the tests into two categories—candidates who might make good officers and those who would do better in some other line of military work. Maybe it wasn't a perfect system, but it had to be better than officer selection based on who could afford to buy a horse, a fancy uniform, and their own commission.

In schools, we use aptitude tests to predict future learning or performance. We use tests of general academic or scholastic ability, those of special abilities (e.g., mechanical ability, readiness for learning, and both ability and previous learning).

Achievement tests, on the other hand, are supposed to measure what a student has learned, or to put it in a more difficult to understand phrase, to measure a student's acquired knowledge and skills in one or more content areas such as reading, mathematics, or science.

Yogi Berra said, "You can see a lot just by looking."

While that might be true for Yogi, it isn't necessarily the case for aptitude and achievement tests. You can't always tell which is which just by looking at the questions. Aptitude tests may or may not differ in content from achievement tests. The difference is in the purpose of the test. Aptitude tests measure intellect and abilities that we don't usually teach in school. They are used to predict future performance—usually in a specific field. Often, aptitude tests are given as individual, as opposed to group, tests.

On the other hand, achievement tests contain items that sample the adequacy of past learning.

Before we go any further, though, we need to mention that achievement tests are not usually designed as precise measures of any given curriculum or single instructional program. Think of your most-used software. Did you buy it "off the shelf"? Does it do everything you'd like for it to do in exactly the way you'd like to have it done? Is it adequate for what you do with it?

Now think about the standardized achievement test you give to your students. Did you buy it "off the shelf" from a major test developer? Do the questions match exactly what you teach when you teach it for every subject in every grade? Is it adequate for what you do with it?

Achievement tests are generally more closely aligned, or matched, with some states' curriculum than with others. Sometimes, you will find that an off-the-shelf achievement test is more aligned with your language arts curriculum than it is with your math curriculum. Or you may find that it's more aligned with the sequence you use for science in middle school than the sequence you use for social studies in the elementary school. So you choose a test that is the best fit all around and you understand that students' scores on the tests should not be used to make life-altering decisions.

NORM-REFERENCED AND CRITERION-REFERENCED TESTS

Question 3 (sort of): Who is Norm, and what does his test reference?

Those of you who answered "Norm was the guy on the TV show *Cheers*, and his test references the number of beers that George Wendt consumed playing him during the 275 episodes *Cheers* aired" may go to the time-out chair until you decide you're ready to pay attention and learn while the rest of us forge ahead.

America's public schools most commonly score standardized tests in one of two ways—norm-referenced scores and criterion-referenced scores. We call these norm-referenced tests (NRTs) and criterion-referenced tests (CRTs) as if there were some prominent mark on each that distinguishes one from the other. Unfortunately, when it comes to seeing an NRT and a CRT, you *still* can't tell by looking.

The key to understanding the difference in an NRT and a CRT is to know to what the students' performance is referenced. NRTs are referenced, or compared, with a representative sample of students who previously took the test. We refer to this administration of the test to a representative sample as "norming" the test and the group as the "norm group." The actual mathematical process for norming goes far beyond the limits of this book (to say nothing of your authors' ability to explain it) so let's just leave it at this—all NRTs measure students' performance in comparison with students in the norm group.

In other words, the results of NRTs give us information that compares a student's achievement with that of a nationwide sample (national norms) or a state or district sample (local norms). The results do not compare a student's achievement with that of other students who took the test at the same time. For example, Sue and Bob both took the test in March 2003. Sue scored in the 84th percentile in mathematics reasoning, while Bob scored in the 60th percentile in mathematics reasoning. Sue's score and Bob's score were compared with the norm group to be ranked, not to each other's scores. Many people believe the student's score is compared with other students' scores who took the test at the same time. This is a common misconception and one we hope you will do your part to eradicate.

NRTs are designed to sort and rank students. They are not precise measures of a student's mastery of a specific curriculum. NRT scores, which we will discuss later, describe a student's position "on the curve" in relationship to the norm group's scores. To make the comparison, the test must be given to a large group for norming.

The norm-referenced tests from national major test developers that you are most likely to encounter in your school career are:

From Harcourt Educational Measurement
- Stanford Achievement Tests
- Metropolitan Achievement Tests

From CTB/McGraw-Hill
- Terra Nova
- Comprehensive Test of Basic Skills
- California Achievement Tests

From Riverside Publishing
- Iowa Test of Basic Skills

Sometimes we don't want to compare a student's performance with some time-distant, probably place-distant, group. What if we want to know whether the student has mastered the necessary skills and knowledge in a particular subject for a particular grade level? Then we need to reference the scores to a set criteria or standard body of knowledge. Criterion-referenced tests (CRTs) are referenced to, or compared with, a body of knowledge and measure students' mastery of that knowledge. The results of CRTs tell us what students have learned relative to a set of standards. CRTs usually rank students' mastery of standards into categories such as Advanced, Proficient, Basic, Below Basic, Novice, Partially Proficient, or categories using similar terms. Students whose scores fall into the lower categories have not mastered the skill that was tested. Sometimes CRTs are reported with a single cut score, such as Mastered/Did Not Master. Students who score above the cut score are considered to have mastered the curriculum; those who score below the cut score have not.

With the advent—or was that avalanche?—of accountability legislation in the various states and at the federal level, the information provided by NRTs is being supplemented, and in some cases replaced by, information provided by CRTs. Schmoker (1999) reminds us that "Criteria-based assessments and rubrics have changed the nature of assessment by providing numerical data that take us beyond the ability to test mere recall. We can now assess understanding, application, and other thinking skills in new ways" (p. 37). That's a good thing.

CRTs are usually specifically developed to align to a set of local or state standards. Unless the cave you live in had a very large rock stuck in its entrance for the last 10 or so years, you've no doubt heard of the work Texas has done to align its state standards and state criterion-referenced tests. The state test, the Texas Assessment of Academic Skills (TAAS) was developed by the Texas Education Agency (TEA) to test the standards as defined by the Essential Elements. TAAS has now been replaced by the Texas Assessment of Knowledge and Skills (TAKS) to test the new standards as defined by the Texas Essential Knowledge and Skills (TEKS). We've told you before—we do not make this stuff up! You can go to the TEA website at www.tea.state.tx.us to watch the evolution of the Texas standards and criterion-referenced testing system.

CRTs are designed to compare a student's test performance with clearly defined curricular objectives, skill levels, or areas of knowledge. Individual scores indicate students' demonstrated mastery of the objectives tested. For example, if a standard for third-grade language arts is that students will learn to distinguish fiction from nonfiction, the criterion-referenced test for that subject and grade might have a story that the students have to read and then decide whether the story is fiction or nonfiction. If the test is seeking to measure skills beyond the knowledge level, the students may also have to explain why the piece is fiction or nonfiction or compare it with another piece of writing. Regardless of the form of the questions, the student responses are measured in the context of what the standards say the student should know. To determine whether a student has mastered a standard, only that one student has to take the test. Or a CRT, like TAKS in Texas, can be given to a particular grade level in the entire state. All 11th-graders must pass TAKS in mathematics, English/language arts, science, and social studies in Texas to graduate from high school. The students are not ranked; there are no norms, because there has been no norm group. Each student's performance is measured to the standard on each objective to determine mastery and a passing score.

Unlike NRTs, which are designed to sort students into performance ranges, it is possible that none, or all, of the CRT examinees will reach a particular goal or performance standard. NRTs produce a range of scores, although it can be a skewed range. Since each student's performance is measured independently against the standard on a CRT, CRTs are useful both to measure student mastery and to refine curriculum and instruction. If a few students do not master a particular concept, then they need additional instruction. If a whole class doesn't master a particular concept, we need to examine whether the concept is being taught to the students. If the concept is being taught, we need to look at how it's being taught. The answers to those and similar questions might lead us to decisions about needed staff development as well as program design and implementation.

"We're lost but we're making good time."

That's another Yogi-ism that is probably more accurate in education than we'd prefer to acknowledge. We give a lot of tests, we collect a lot of data, and we still don't know where we're going, or how we got to where we are now. To paraphrase a statement attributed to Grant Wiggins, we spend a lot of time waving from the dock (Schmoker 1999, 37). You should not be surprised to find, given the long lists of questions in the first part of this handbook, that we suggest you know which questions you want to answer before you decide which tests to give. Are you testing for accountability reporting? Do you want to compare the achievement of your students with the achievement of others in the same grade at the same time of year? Do you want to determine whether your students have mastered a particular algebraic concept? What information do you want from the test? Who will use the information you get? Answering those questions before you even think about asking, "Which test should you give?" is the first step to giving the right test for your purposes.

Table 10.1 summarizes the uses of NRTs and CRTs in schools and districts.

Table 10.1. Uses of NRTs and CRTs in Schools and Districts

Why do we need to test?	*kind of test do we need?*	*Who will use the resulting data?*
We want to compare achievement of local students with achievement of students in the nation, state, or other districts in a given year.	NRT	School board, superintendent, central office staff, parents, community (e.g., chamber of commerce, realtors' association)
We want to compare achievement of subgroups of local students with achievement of similar subgroups in the nation, state, or other districts in a given year.	NRT	Central office staff, program directors
We want to compare achievement of one student subgroup (e.g., sex, race, or age) with achievement of another such subgroup in a given year to determine the equity of educational outcomes.	NRT	Central office staff, program directors, principals
We want to assess the extent to which students in a single grade (at district, building, or classroom level) have mastered the essential objectives of the school system's curriculum.	CRT	Program directors, curriculum coordinators, principals, teachers

(continued)

(Table 10.1. continued)

Why do we need to test?	kind of test do we need?	Who will use the resulting data?
We want to assess the extent to which a given student is learning the essential objectives of the school system's curriculum and, subsequently, to adjust instruction for that student.	CRT	Principals, teachers, parents
We want to follow achievement of a cohort of students through the system or area to determine the extent to which their mastery of the curriculum improves over time.	CRT	Program directors, curriculum coordinators, principals, teachers
We want to follow achievement of a cohort of students in a given school to determine the extent to which they learn essential objectives of school system's curriculum.	CRT	Principals, teachers

Note: Adapted from Rudner, L. M., and Conoley, J. C., Ed. (1998) *Understanding Achievement.*

Compiled by ERIC Clearinghouse on Tests, Measurement, and Evaluation, American Institutes for Research; Buros Institute of Mental Measurements, University of Nebraska–Lincoln.

11

Here Are Your Scores

> The key is to think of data as a learning tool. We use data to test
> the theories of ideas. (Conzemius and O'Neill 2002, 62)

Now that you have acquired a working knowledge of standardized tests,
you're ready to move from giving the test to understanding the results.
Scores are reported in a variety of ways and are often calculated using a
variety of proprietary methods. That is, the scorer came up with the

method and wants to sell it to you, not give it to you free. In this chapter we'll focus on the basic scores that are most commonly used and frequently available throughout the country in reporting standardized test scores.

RAW SCORES

A raw score is the number of items answered correctly on any given test or subtest in a content area. That's the fancy way of saying that the raw score is how many you got right. Suppose two fifth-grade students take the same teacher-made math test. John correctly answers 15 of the 30 questions and Joe correctly answers 20 of the 30. John's raw score is 15; Joe's is 20. You could logically assume that Joe had a better grasp of math. Your logic might not be all you think it is. You can't tell anything about the questions from the raw score. You don't know how hard the questions were. Without examining the test, you don't even know if a high score actually measures math mastery.

It gets worse—what if John correctly answers 15 of 30 questions on a math test and 20 of 30 on a reading test? Does that mean he is better at reading than at math? Maybe, but we can't tell by looking at the raw scores. We don't know which test is the more difficult of the two or even at what point in the school year the tests were given.

Obviously, if one student's raw score is 1 out of a possible 50 and another student's score is 49 out of a possible 50 on the same test, you can probably be more comfortable with student two's subject mastery.

Raw scores have limited utility for analyzing large groups of scores. You should never use them to compare achievement from grade to grade, from test to test, or from one subject to another. However, raw scores are certainly useful to individual students in determining how much of the content they mastered, especially when they look at their own test papers and see exactly which problems they missed and which they got right. In the standardized test world, you may find raw scores reported on both NRTs and CRTs. But there's not much you can conveniently do with them.

PERCENT CORRECT SCORES

If looking at the actual number of items that a student answers correctly is somewhat limited, what about computing the total percent correct score? The total percent correct score is found by dividing the total number of items by the number of correct answers. If a test had 10 items and the student answered 5 correct, then 5 divided by 10 is 50 percent correct. The same is true for a 100-item test on which the student got 50 items right: 50 divided by 100 equals 50 percent right. So, 50 percent is 50 percent, right?

Again you are faced with the problem that you can't tell the test rigor or item difficulty, or for that matter even the number of items on the test, just by looking at the score. You can use them to get some notion of whether a student missed half the items on a test or three-fourths or one-fourth, but percent correct scores are of limited utility in comparing student achievement. You can't use percent correct scores for comparing achievement from grade to grade, test to test, or subject to subject either. You may find percent correct scores reported on both NRTs and CRTs.

PERCENTILE RANK

Finally, here's one we all know and understand. Everyone has seen and understands percentile rank, don't they? Percentile rank is an often used and extremely precise measure of student achievement, right? Often used, maybe. Precise, not hardly.

Percentile rank scores are the darlings of the media. Headlines exclaim that "Ninety percent of students scored above the 50th percentile" or "Most scores fall below the 50th percentile." Most people read the headline and think they know exactly what it means. Some of these people are right.

If a student scored at the 82nd percentile, the student's score ranked higher than 81 percent of all of the scores of the students who took the same norm-referenced test during the norming process. Read that sentence again. The student's score is not compared with the scores of the students who took the test at the same time the student took the test, it's compared with the scores of the norm group. The student's score doesn't mean he or she got 82 percent of the questions right. It does mean that the student's score, in comparison with the scores of the norm group, was near the top end of the range of scores, ranking higher than 81 percent of the norm group.

That point may bear repeating as we've known people to confuse this issue. If a student's score is at a percentile rank, that score indicates that whatever his or her score was, it was higher than that of the norm group students who answered fewer questions correctly. That rank does not equate to a certain percent correct.

If the score is called a national percentile rank (NPR), the norm group consisted of a representative sample of students in the nation at the time the test was normed. This means that the norm group for the test was representative of students in the same grade at the same time of year across the entire nation. Your district may use regionally or locally normed tests in your school system as well.

Information should be available from the publisher on the norming process and the norm group. The norming process is expensive and time-consuming, so tests are not normed each year. Renorming is done on a periodic basis. When a test is renormed, you must get the new version of the test with the new norms, or your scoring is invalid. The date your test was normed can have an impact on your scores. Are you using a test that was normed eight years ago? Have your teachers learned enough about the test that they are unconsciously teaching more of the content that they know will be tested? Do you still teach the content in the same sequence? Do you use calculators in your math instruction but a test that does not allow their use? All of these issues and more can have either positive or negative impacts on your test scores independent of your course content or instructional methods. This information is in the publisher's information book.

The graphic representation of the national percentile rank scores of a population is the bell-shaped curve. On the bell-shaped curve, the scores in the middle (under that big hump) are more closely clustered together than the scores at either end of the curve. Technically speaking, the curve really represents the percent of scores in the area under the curve. Think of a row of blocks stacked vertically with their sides touching each other. Looking from left to right, the first block is the 2-percent-of-all-the-scores block, the next is the 14-percent-of-all-the-scores block, and the third is the 34-percent-of-all-the-scores block. If you were adding the blocks together, you realize we now have blocks that represent 50 percent of the scores. If we keep going to the right we have another 34 percent block, another 14 percent block and another 2 percent block. Now we have 100 percent of the scores. If you were to drape a shoestring across the top of the blocks—voila!—a normal curve.

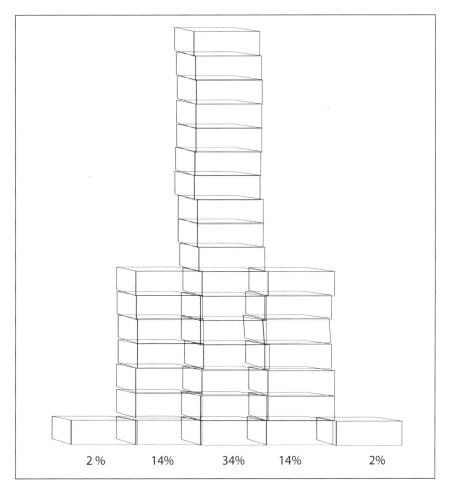

| 2 % | 14% | 34% | 14% | 2% |

Look back at the blocks. The width of each block is the same. But the first block on the left represents scores approximately up to the 2nd percentile; the second block represents scores between the 2nd percentile and the 16th percentile and the third block represents the scores between the

16th percentile and the 50th. Obviously, there are a lot more scores crowded together on the top of that last block than are on the first one. If the tops of the blocks are the same width, there has to be more space between scores on the top of the first block than there is between scores on the top of the third. In other words, the scores are not equal-interval scores. The distance between the scores is not equal.

Since NPRs are not equal-interval scores, they have different meanings at different places. Why did we go through all that playing with blocks? We wanted to make this very important point: A gain of 5 percentile points is actually much larger if it occurs at either end of the distribution than if it occurs in the middle.

Therefore, percentile ranks cannot legitimately be added, subtracted, or averaged. And it shouldn't be done illegitimately either! Santa Claus. The tooth fairy. Average percentile rank. Not real.

Percentile rank scores are reported on NRTs. That should make sense to you at this point. If a score on a test is referenced to a norm, and you're reporting a score that indicates a student's rank in relation to the norm group, then you can report a score to correspond to that rank. Recently we have seen percentile rank scores reported for some CRTs. If you run into a CRT with percentile rank scores, we suggest you ask the following questions: Was the test normed? To what norm group? May you see the documentation? If it was normed, then it may be appropriate to have percentile rank scores reported for that CRT. If not, then you shouldn't report percentile rank scores on a CRT because there is nothing against which to rank scores. As we said earlier, you can't tell by looking at the test—what makes a percentile rank possible is the norming process.

That leads us to one point on our "they are not as accurate as you think they are" soapbox. We will now stand on our soapbox to lecture for a moment—there are a lot of variables that can affect test scores. Just because test scores are numbers—or worse yet, numbers with two decimal places-it doesn't mean they are "carved in stone" accurate and that they should be used exclusively to make instructional decisions. A test score can be one piece of the puzzle. Remember that just because a puzzle piece is blue, it doesn't have to be a part of the sky. In chapter 8 we talked about Victoria Bernhardt's idea of triangulation, using at least three data points to make decisions. We think it is wise to include test scores as *one* data point, not *the* data point.

One more step up onto the soapbox—a word about precision. Just because numbers have a decimal point and one, two, three, or four places to the right of that decimal point does not mean that a score is a precise measure of a student's achievement. One score, regardless of the decimal places, is not the "be all to end all" score. Students' scores can vary depending on the time of day, the day of the week, whether the wind is blowing, whether they spent all weekend cooped up in the house, whether the student is coming down with a cold, and a variety of other factors. Again, we repeat—you should not use any one score to make potentially life-altering decisions about a student's future. We will climb down from our soapbox now.

SCALED SCORES

Our apologies—we're all about tests here and we haven't given you one lately. Let's clear up that grievous oversight right now.

Question 4: Scaled scores measure which of the following?
   A. The difference between what you weigh on your bathroom scales and on your doctor's scales.
   B. Points collected at a bass tournament.
   C. Equal-interval scores on a single scale.
   Answer: Surely we don't even have to tell you that the answer is C!

But we suppose you do want us to tell you what that means. Here goes.

Remember all those bad things we had to say about raw scores—about how you can't use them to measure item difficulty or to compare tests? Well, scaling is the statistical procedure that overcomes those deficiencies. In the simplest of terms, scaling is a method of conversion. Just as the amount of coffee you drink in a day may be expressed in terms of liters or gallons, scores can be expressed on different scales. The use of a different scale to express the scores doesn't change the value of the score (you still drink *a lot* of coffee!) but it does make the scores more useful for certain types of comparisons.

Scaled scores are scores on a single scale (e.g., 1–100 or 526–634) with intervals of equal size. Unlike raw scores, scaled scores take into account the relative difficulty of the test items through the use of a mathematical formula. Using the scaled scores, you can compare scores within a content area from level to level and form to form. Because the scores are equal-interval scores, you can add, subtract, and average them across levels within a content area. You can compare the average scaled score in third-grade math with the average scaled score in fourth-grade math.

What you can't do is use scaled scores to compare one content area with another. You can't compare the average scaled score in third-grade math with the average scaled score in fourth-grade science. Well, strictly speaking, we suppose you can, and, in fact, your information might appear to be correct and your chart might be beautiful, but someone in the audience will know you've used the scores incorrectly and there goes your credibility! Not to mention the fact that the information is useless for decision-making.

On the flip side, scaled scores don't give an individual student information about his or her achievement level unless he or she knows the score range. A student scored 379 on a fifth-grade math test. Is that good or bad? There's no way to tell unless you know the range of possible scores. If your average test score is 793, is that good, bad, or indifferent? If the score is for the math portion of the SAT, then it's pretty impressive. If it's your composite score for both the math and the verbal parts, then you don't want to be counting too heavily on that academic scholarship. The same caution applies to group scores.

Scaled scores are reported on both NRTs and CRTs. We'll discuss scaled scores in more detail when we talk about CRT cut scores and performance levels.

NORMAL CURVE EQUIVALENT

Question 5: A normal curve equivalent score is which of the following?
    A. An equal-interval score.
    B. A normalized standard score that is equivalent to a point on the normal curve.
    C. A score that can be added, subtracted, and averaged.
    D. All of the above.
    Answer: D, of course.

The normal curve equivalent (NCE) is a means of measuring the spot where a student's score falls along the normal curve. But wait, isn't that what a percentile rank score does? Yes, but NCEs have a very important advantage over NPRs. NCEs can be averaged. Therefore, you can use NCEs to compute group statistics, measure school performance, and document schoolwide or classwide gains and losses in student achievement. The numbers on the NCE run from 1 to 99, with 50 as the average. Those points on the normal curve line match, or are equivalent to, those same points—1, 99, and 50—along the percentile score line.

The formula for converting a percentile score to an NCE is $50 + 21.06(z)$. The "z" represents the z-score. You get the z-score by subtracting the arithmetic mean of all the raw scores from a particular raw score and dividing the sum by the standard deviation of all the raw scores. Knowing all of that should make you really glad to know this handbook contains a conversion table (table 11.1) to help you match up scores—you don't have to do the calculations yourself unless you really, really want to.

Table 11.1.   National Percentile Rank (NPR)-to-Normal Curve Equivalent (NCE) Conversion

NPR	NCE	NPR	NCE
1	1	51	50.52803
2	6.741673	52	51.0564
3	10.38472	53	51.58542
4	13.1251	54	52.11544
5	15.35428	55	52.64682
6	17.25166	56	53.17988
7	18.91524	57	53.71498
8	20.40477	58	54.25252
9	21.75954	59	54.79281
10	23.00655	60	55.33627
11	24.16549	61	55.88334
12	25.25111	62	56.43438
13	26.2747	63	56.98988
14	27.24509	64	57.55027
15	28.1695	65	58.11606
16	29.05363	66	58.68775
17	29.90233	67	59.26595
18	30.71955	68	59.85119
19	31.50877	69	60.44414
20	32.27283	70	61.04552
21	33.01425	71	61.656
22	33.73522	72	62.27644
23	34.4376	73	62.90775
24	35.12308	74	63.55084
25	35.79313	75	64.20687
26	36.44916	76	64.87692

(continued)

(Table 11.1. continued)

NPR	NCE	NPR	NCE
27	37.09225	77	65.5624
28	37.72356	78	66.26478
29	38.344	79	66.98575
30	38.95448	80	67.72717
31	39.55586	81	68.49123
32	40.14881	82	69.28045
33	40.73405	83	70.09767
34	41.31225	84	70.94637
35	41.88394	85	71.8305
36	42.44973	86	72.75491
37	43.01012	87	73.7253
38	43.56562	88	74.74889
39	44.11666	89	75.83451
40	44.66373	90	76.99345
41	45.20719	91	78.24046
42	45.74748	92	79.59523
43	46.28502	93	81.08476
44	46.82012	94	82.74834
45	47.35318	95	84.64572
46	47.88456	96	86.8749
47	48.41458	97	89.61528
48	48.9436	98	93.25833
49	49.47197	99	99
50	50		

The nice thing about NCEs is that you can use them to compare the performance of students who take different levels or forms of the same test within a test battery, e.g., Terra Nova Mathematics Grade 4 and Terra Nova Mathematics Grade 5. You can also use them to evaluate gains over time and draw comparisons across subject matter for the same student. Best of all, you can use them to compute meaningful summary statistics. Although you can't compute an average NPR, you can compute an average NCE.

You may want to keep table 11.1 handy, however, as NCEs don't give you easily understood information about an individual student's achievement level unless you compare the score with another value or convert it to a percentile rank.

NCEs are reported for NRTs. We've also heard NCEs called normalized standard scores. While they are normalized standard scores, they are not the only kind of normalized standard scores.

STANINE

A stanine is another type of normalized standard score that is also often reported on NRTs. A stanine is the unit of a standard score scale that divides the normal population into nine groups. The word *stanine* comes from the fact that it is a STAndard score on a scale of NINE units. On the stanine scale, 1 is the lowest score while 9 is the highest. Like percentile ranks, stanines are used to indicate a student's achievement level in reference to a norm group. Stanines 1, 2, and 3 are usually considered below average; while 4, 5, and 6 are considered average; and 7, 8, and 9, above average.

Stanines show the standing of students in relation to the national or local average. They are easy to explain and they can be used to group students into performance groups. The limitation of stanines is that there are only nine scores to correspond to a wide range of percentile rank scores. Thus stanines are not particularly precise and are of limited utility. If a student's score is a stanine of 3 one year and a stanine of 3 the following year, the student could have improved but the stanine score, because it encompasses such a relatively broad range of percentile rank scores, would not reflect any improvement. On the other hand, a difference of two stanines might signal a real difference.

GRADE EQUIVALENTS

NRT scores are also often reported as grade equivalents (GE). A grade equivalent is based on a 10-month school year and indicates the grade and month of the school year for which a given score is the actual or estimated average. For example, if a student scores at the average of all sixth-graders tested in the second month of the school year, he would obtain a GE of 6.2. On the other hand, if the student's score were the same as the average for all sixth-graders tested in the ninth month, the grade equivalent would be 6.9.

Question 6: Suppose the student who scored the 6.9 was actually in the second month of the third grade. Does the 6.9 score mean that the student should be sent to sixth grade for math instruction?
  A. No.
  B. Not really.
  C. Absolutely not.
  D. Don't even think about it.
  E. All of the above.
  Answer: E. You should use great care in interpreting GE scores.

What a GE of 6.9 means for the student in third grade is that she performed as well as the real or estimated average of all sixth-grade students tested in the ninth month of the school year on that test. Probably the student is a good math student.

At the same time, a sixth-grade child whose grade equivalent score on the math subtest is 3.9 should not necessarily be changed to a third-grade math class. These scores, like all data, should be used to highlight issues, not to make instant decisions. If you find a third-grade math teacher whose students consistently score a grade level or two above their peers, you might want to find out what good things are happening in that class.

You might assume that a series of scores, e.g., 3.2, 4.2, 5.2, 6.2, indicates a year's growth at each interval. While that assumption seems intuitive, it is not correct. The expected growth in reading, for example, decreases between grades over time and varies increasingly with student age. Not only that, but the formula behind the computation of GE scales is a lot more complicated than we would even vaguely consider trying to explain. Suffice it to say that the scale is not linear nor of equal intervals and therefore grade equivalents cannot be added, subtracted, or averaged across test levels. If all that is not enough to convince you to treat GE scores with great caution, keep in mind that every GE score is unique to its test, so you can't use them to compare one test with another, either.

Last, but not least, remember that the student's GE, like the NPR, NCE, and stanine is related to the scores of the norming group, not the scores of other students who took the test at the same time.

SCORES REPORTED FOR CRT

Most CRT score reports include scaled scores, cut scores, and scoring levels. We discussed scaled scores earlier. A range of scaled scores represents a scoring level. Cut scores are the scaled scores that divide the scores into ranges. It works like this: Suppose you have a fifth-grade language arts CRT with a range of possible scaled scores of 437 to 576. Within that range there are "cuts" or scores that define each performance level. For example, a student whose scaled score falls between 437 and 478 has a score at the Novice level. The student who scores between 479 and 523 performs at the Adequate level. A score of 524 to 551 is Proficient; 552 to 576 is Advanced. In this example, 479, 524, and 552 are cut scores—they form the boundary between two ranges. Scores below those levels fall into one category; scores above those levels fall into the next higher category. Table 11.2 also illustrates these levels.

Table 11.2.

Performance Level	Cut Score	Range
Advanced	552	552–576
Proficient	524	524–551
Adequate	479	479–523
Novice	437*	437–478

Note: In this example, 437 is the lowest score a student can make on the fifth-grade test.

These scores are sometimes called criterion scores. A student who scores 524 in the above example meets the criterion for Proficient; a student who scores 523 does not.

On most CRTs, scaled score ranges and cut scores differ from test to test and grade to grade. Cut scores are usually set by a panel of subject-matter experts who score assessments in a structured collective setting to establish the ranges for the various performance levels.

12

Turning Scores into Information

> Discovery consists of seeing what everybody has seen and thinking what nobody has thought. (Albert von Szent-Gyorgyi, 1893–1986)

As you begin to look at your test data and analyze numbers, you will need a basic understanding of descriptive statistics. The people with whom you'll be sharing your data need to understand them as well. For instance, suppose you want to establish the "average" test score for a certain grade level. Does everyone understand "average" in the same way? To most people, average is the mean, or arithmetic average. To mathematicians and those who have studied statistics, average can be the mean, median, or mode. Others will ask that you average ordinal numbers. Let's explore these issues and some other measures, too.

AVERAGES

Yes, the mean, median, and mode are all averages. They are all measures of central tendency. On a normal curve they are all at the 50th percentile. And they are all different from one another.

MEAN

The mean is the arithmetic average of a set of scores. You find the mean by adding all the scores in the distribution and dividing by the total number of scores. You can use the mean to describe interval or ratio data. The mean is easy to calculate and easy to understand. Using mean, however, might not accurately reflect your average test score.

For example, consider whether the mean most accurately reports the results of the following survey.

Ask seven teachers in your school how much money they are carrying. The results might look like those in table 12.1.

Table 12.1.

Teacher	Amount
Martina	$3.00
Pierre	$2.00
Amy	$1.00
Donnie	$10.00
Juan	$5.00
Russ	$2.00
Jim	$999.00
Total	$1022.00

If you use the mean ($146) as the average, then it will look as if your teachers bring a lot of money to school. In fact, most of them bring very little, but the one high number has a very significant effect on the average when you use the mean. The same thing can happen with test scores. You may have a lot of students who score toward the low end of a range of scores and a few students who score at the very top end of the range. If you create a mean, you could "hide" those scores on the lower end.

To further complicate matters, the mean is often not a "real number." None of us has ever had 2.3 children, even if that was the average number in the United States at one time. In the example in table 12.1, no one actually had $146. When you create a test score report and include an average score, you may find that it's not a real score at all.

Occasionally, you will find a mean reported that not only isn't real, it's entirely meaningless as well. Here's how that can happen. Ordinal data is totally different from interval data. With interval data one number can be compared with another's value—four peaches are twice as much as two. That's an interval. Ordinal numbers don't work like that. For example, what's the ranking of your favorite college football team? If your team is No. 5 in the top 10, does that mean they are only half as good as the No. 1 ranked team? Or twice as good as No. 10? Of course not—rank indicates relative position, not intervals. That is the difference between ordinal data and interval data.

Suppose the teachers in our previous example decided to conduct a taste test with three drinks (Jim has offered to buy). They each taste the drinks and rank them on a scale of 1 to 3 for tartness, with 3 being the most tart. The results are shown in table 12.2:

Table 12.2.

	Lemonade	Orangeade	Limeade
Martina	1	2	3
Donnie	1	3	2
Juan	2	3	1
Amy	3	2	1
Russ	1	3	2
Pierre	1	2	3
Jim	2	1	3

Our results are in the form of ordinal, not interval or ratio, data. Our teachers ranked the drinks. Martina thought Orangeade was tarter than Lemonade but less tart than Limeade. But her ranking doesn't indicate that she thinks Orangeade is twice as tart as Lemonade. Jim doesn't think

Lemonade is twice as tart as Orangeade. So if were to take the various scores and create a mean, we would report that the "average" tartness of Lemonade was 1.57, that of Orangeade 2.28, and that of Limeade 2.14—altogether totally meaningless means. That is one way to get a mean that isn't real and is totally without value.

So how do you report your results for ordinal data? The frequency distribution in table 12.3 is one example. A frequency distribution simply counts the number of times a certain score was given for each choice, something like tally marks.

Table 12.3.

Lemonade Tartness Score	Frequency of Score
1	4
2	2
3	1

MEDIAN

Another way to report the results of the taste test is to use the median. The median is the middle score in a distribution or set of ranked scores. The best way to describe ordinal data is to use the median. To find the median, rank the scores from low to high (or high to low) and find the score in the middle. Half the scores are below the median, and half are above it. The median is the point (score) that divides a group into two equal parts. In a normal curve, the median is 50th percentile. Using our taste-test example, let's rank the scores (table 12.4) and determine the medians.

Table 12.4.

Lemonade	Orangeade	Limeade
1	1	1
1	2	1
1	2	2
1	2	2
2	3	3
2	3	3
3	3	3
Median = 1	Median = 2	Median = 2

That makes a lot more sense!

The median can also be used to describe the interval data in our earlier money survey. The median in that example is $3. The median is more representative of the fact that most of the teachers don't bring a lot of money to school. Using the median might also better describe your situation if you have many students who score toward the low end of a range of scores and a few students who score at the very top end of the range on a test. A median might give a truer picture of your scores.

One more important thing about a median—if you have an even number of scores, to determine the median you add the two in the middle and divide by two.

For example, scores on a math test, ranked from highest to lowest, are 40, 14, 6, and 4. The median is (14 + 6) / 2, or 10. The mean is 16, found by adding the numbers together and dividing by 4. The median gives a more accurate picture of the "central tendency" of the scores as not being very high.

MODE

The last measure of central tendency we will discuss is the mode. The mode is the score or value that occurs most frequently in a distribution. The nice thing about the mode is that there's no calculation involved. You just look at the scores, find the one that you see the most often and that's the mode. In a normal curve, the mode is at the 50th percentile. In a non-normal curve, however, you might have two modes (a bimodal curve) so you can see how that might not be too useful in describing central tendency. The only time that you absolutely have to use the mode and nothing else is when you are describing nominal data. Nominal data are names, and you must use the mode because you can't use anything median or mean, since you can't perform mathematical functions on names. For example, let's check table 12.5 to see which fruit our teachers brought for lunch.

Table 12.5.

Teacher	Lunch Fruit
Martina	Apple
Donnie	Orange
Juan	Peach
Amy	Apple
Russ	Apple
Pierre	Orange
Jim	Strawberries

The mode is? Apple!

VARIABILITY

Mean, median, and mode are measures of central tendency. Range, variance, and standard deviation are measures of variability. As important as it is for you to know the mean of your scores, it is also important that you know how much the scores vary around that particular mean. This is where measures of variability come into the discussion.

Range

The range is the difference between the lowest score and the highest score (or the highest score and the lowest score) once the scores are arranged in order. You determine the range by subtracting the lowest number from the highest one. Remember the teachers' money example? The range is 998 ($999–$1). Easy to calculate but not too helpful if that's the only number you have when you need to analyze your data. The range of amounts from $10,999 to $10,001 would also be 998 but the "scores" are certainly different.

Variance

Another measure of variability, variance indicates the amount of spread in the scores. If the scores are clustered together, the variance is small. If the scores are spread out over a large range, the variance is large. You can calculate variance fairly easily—start by subtracting each score from the mean. If you have scores of 78, 75, 72, 67, 64, 59, and 43, the mean is 65. The first calculations look like this:

- 78 – 65 = 13
- 75 – 65 = 10
- 72 – 65 = 7
- 67 – 65 = 2
- 64 – 65 = –1
- 59 – 65 = –6
- 43 – 65 = –22

The next step is to square each difference and add the answers together.

- 13 × 13 = 169
- 10 × 10 = 100
- 7 × 7 = 49
- 2 × 2 = 4
- 1 × –1 = 1
- –6 × –6 = 36
- –22 × –22 = 484
- 169 + 100 + 49 + 4 + 1 + 36 + 484 = 843

Next, divide the squared differences (843) by the number of scores (7). The result, 120.42, is the variance of the scores.

Now that we've done the calculation, we would first like to express our profound gratitude to the person who invented the portable calculator. Then we need to say that the variance alone doesn't give us much information.

That's the second time we've said that in this section. At this point you may be thinking, "If the range doesn't tell me much and the variance doesn't tell me much, why am I reading this book?" Hang on. Here comes the big one.

Standard Deviation

Using the variance we found above (120.42), we can determine the standard deviation (SD). To determine the standard deviation, we calculate the square root of 120.42. That's 10.97. There are, of course, ways to calculate the square root of a number without a graphing calculator. Our favorite if we need a quick calculation, however, is to go to www.Math.com and use its square root calculator.

The standard deviation is a measure of dispersion. The more scores cluster around the mean, the smaller the standard deviation.

Standard deviation is in fact another kind of average—the average difference among the individual scores in a group of scores and the mean of that set of scores. If you know the mean of your test scores and the standard deviation, you're well on your way to using descriptive statistics to turn your data into information.

While the size of the standard deviation does not depend greatly on extreme scores, the more scores are spread out from the mean, the larger the size of the standard deviation. Conversely, the more the scores cluster around the mean, the smaller the standard deviation. In a normal distribution of scores, 68.3% of the scores are within the range of one SD below the mean to one SD above the mean.

Good practice dictates that whenever you report the mean, you also report the standard deviation (Carroll and Carroll 2002, 48). Consider the example in table 12.6, which includes the means and the standard deviations of the complete battery of an NRT given four years in grades 2 through 10. If we focus only on the means, we note that the mean score has increased in each grade every year. This appears to be a positive trend. However, let's not drag out those laurels to rest on just yet.

Look next at the standard deviations. Remember that the larger the SD, the more the scores vary around the mean. Does the slightly larger standard deviation for the 2000–2001 school year indicate that students at the top end of the scoring scale are progressing while those at the lower end are not? Maybe. Maybe not. This is just another place where one answer generates more than one question. We would need to dig more deeply into the scores, for instance disaggregating by subgroup, to determine exactly what is happening with these scores.

Table 12.6.

	1997–1998	1997–1998	1998–1999	1998–1999	1999–2000	1999–2000	2000–2001	2000–2001
	Mean	Standard Deviation	Mean	Standard Deviation	Mean	Standard Deviation	Mean	Standard Deviation
Grade 2	41.39	9.98	44.07	10.02	46.66	10.73	49.72	11.26
Grade 3	41.12	10.14	44.18	10.27	46.69	10.85	49.33	11.56
Grade 4	40.66	10.06	44.12	10.59	46.84	10.7	50	11.3
Grade 5	41.72	9.86	43.31	10.54	46.84	11.47	49.54	11.4
Grade 6	40.91	9.67	44.09	10.32	46.51	10.95	49.91	12.2
Grade 7	41.33	9.45	43.72	10.19	46.3	10.88	49.18	11.66
Grade 8	41.37	9.83	44.28	9.87	46.55	10.63	49.39	11.31
Grade 9	41.19	9.83	43.97	10.38	46.98	10.49	49.06	11.1
Grade 10	41.53	9.52	44.6	10.19	46.9	10.73	49.82	11.08

CROSS-SECTIONAL AND LONGITUDINAL ANALYSIS

We can't stress enough that you should not make major curriculum and instructional decisions based on one or two sets of numbers or a few test scores. Rather, you should be looking at patterns and trends in your data over time.

Data-driven decision-making is at its most powerful when we find trends and patterns as the basis to determine causes and address those causes. Therefore, you must be able to use any data-analysis system to compare data over time, preferably with a matched longitudinal method, along with unmatched longitudinal data and cross-sectional data.

One way you can view your student data is to look at information about students in one class, grade, or program and compare them to students in another class, grade, or program. This method is called "cross-sectional" analysis. If you compare the standardized test scores of the third grade in 2001–2002 with the standardized test scores of the fourth grade in 2001–2002, you are performing a cross-sectional analysis. Such analysis is used quite commonly, even currently required by federal law, but is not very powerful for looking at individual student progress. Nor is it very helpful in diagnosing problems with curriculum and instructional methods. It also leads to short-term thinking, rather than looking at long-term trends and patterns.

A much better way to view the performance of students and teachers, is to use longitudinal analysis—follow a group of students over time as they move through your school system. If you compare the standardized test scores of the third grade in 2001–2002 with the standardized test scores of the fourth grade in 2002–2003, you are performing a longitudinal analysis. A longitudinal analysis allows you to look at students' performance over time as they move through the district's curriculum. It allows you to see if the group is gaining, losing, or staying even in their performance.

To follow exactly the same students, you use matched longitudinal analysis.

For example, a third-grade group includes Johnny Jones, Suzie Smith, and Carrie Curtis. Johnny Jones moves away during the summer; Rita Russell moves in. Neither Johnny's test scores nor Rita's test scores would be included in your matched longitudinal analysis.

A careful analysis of Suzie, Carrie, and the other students who were in your school in both third and fourth grades should indicate whether they are making reasonable progress as they move from grade to grade. Using this matched approach, you generally get the best picture of how your various programs, curriculum, and methods of instruction impact student learning.

With the recent focus on accountability, some are tempted to measure a teacher's performance by the students' performance in his room one year. A better measure is to look at the value added in his classroom over time. You can do this by measuring the students' achievement prior to entering his classroom, then again upon exiting his classroom, and figuring the gain in achievement. Doing this yearly begins to give a pattern of value added that helps in making decisions about staff development, mentoring, and teacher assistance.

VARIATION

As you look at your information over time, keep in mind the concept of variation. Variation is normal and expected in any system and can be illustrated by a very common example. When we ask you what you weigh, you reply "150 pounds." (Although, because we are southern ladies, we promise we would absolutely never, never ask you that question!) In fact, if you weigh daily, you might find your weight varies like this:

- Sunday—153
- Monday—151
- Tuesday—152
- Wednesday—150
- Thursday—149
- Friday—148
- Saturday—150

No problem. You expect variation in your daily weight. Variation is normal. How long does it take you to drive to work? Fifteen minutes? It varies, based on traffic, weather, and whether you hit the traffic light on red or green. The same is true with data—variation is normal. Don't get caught up in trying to analyze small changes in individual test scores or any other performance indicator. You'll spend a lot of time and won't know much when you're finished.

CORRELATION IS NOT CAUSATION

Obviously, all schools collect more information about students than their test scores. We discussed many possibilities earlier in this book. We've suggested that you compare some of that information with test scores or with other information. For instance, do students who have a high number of absences have lower test scores than those who have near-perfect attendance? Do students who have discipline referrals for violating a particular school rule perform less well on one type of test than they do on another?

As you begin to look at data that answers these types of questions, you might see relationships and begin to form conclusions about individual students or groups of students. *Stop! Don't!* There is a large difference between realizing that a relationship exists and knowing what causes that relationship.

Relationships between sets of data can be weak or strong, positive or negative. You can use the Pearson *r* correlation coefficient to determine the magnitude of the association or to detect the direction (+ or –). The closer the correlation to 1.0, the stronger the association, so –.75 and +.75 are equally strong relationships. The negative simply indicates that as one variable goes down, the other goes up. The positive correlation indicates that both variables go in the same direction; that direction could be up or down.

You can also use correlations as a foundation for more sophisticated statistics. What you cannot, and in fact *must not*, do is to confuse correlation with causation.

Suppose that in recent years your state legislature has reduced the funds it allocated for your state's department of natural resources. Natural resources officers patrol your state's lakes, issuing citations for speedboat violations. Because of the budget cuts, the department has fewer offices patrolling the lakes. You decide to conduct a study of the drownings in your state lakes, and you discover that the number has increased in recent years. In fact, you find a high correlation between the number of drownings and the budget cuts. Does that mean that budget cuts caused the drownings? No, drowning is caused by water filling the lungs. But you can say that there appears to be a relationship between budget cuts and the number of drownings. You might even conclude that the decrease in the number of law enforcement officers on the lakes citing safety violations is highly correlated with the increase in the number of drownings. But it's still water in the lungs that causes people to drown.

By the same token, just because a student misses school and scores poorly on tests doesn't necessarily mean that the poor attendance causes the low test scores. Nor can you conclude that the low test scores could cause the poor attendance. Both the poor attendance and the low test scores could stem from some other cause. Maybe the student has a chronic illness, causing both the poor attendance and the low test scores. Or maybe not. You just don't know the cause.

What you can do is recognize that there is a relationship and work to improve one or both of the variables (test scores and attendance). You can continue to study to better try to understand the cause or causes, because many times there is more than one cause. And you can understand that correlation is not causation, something that many people do not understand.

NOT INFERENTIAL STATISTICS

This has been a short discussion of test scores and measures most commonly used to discuss student performance. We know there are others, but we'd rather you felt comfortable with the few most important commonly used ones than confused by a lot.

We have also not included any inferential statistics in our discussions. If you are looking at your whole population of students, you don't need to infer.

You use inferential statistics when you have a sample of a population and you want to infer characteristics of the whole population based on what you know about the sample. When political pollsters predict election results, they don't question every single person who voted; they question a sample and use inferential statistics to predict how the entire population will vote. If you've collected your data correctly and built your warehouse correctly, you have the entire universe of your data.

If you are looking at a student, you have the data on that student. If you are looking at a class, you have the data on that class. If you are looking at a grade level, you have the data on that grade level. The same is true for an identified student group, a school, or a district. In each case, you have the entire population, so no inference is needed.

STATISTICAL SIGNIFICANCE

We promise this will be the last of our lectures, but we just have to say something about statistical significance. Findings that are statistically significant might have zero practical import. Findings that are not statistically significant might be vitally important.

A test for statistical significance is only a statement of odds, not of program impact. A test of statistical significance tells you only how likely it is that a difference of that magnitude could have occurred by chance. If you test everyone in the district and the district is the only universe of interest, then there is no point in running a test of significance: The difference is real no matter how large or small it might be (Bracey 2000, 59).

Often you will hear the comments "the score is only one standard deviation away from the mean" or "the difference in the scores is not significant." Statistically speaking, those comments are correct. In the academic life of a child, these phrases have no place. Each child is significant; each child's progress is significant.

Part 4

SO WHAT?

In part 1, we worked with the process of looking at your goals, asking questions about your goals, gathering data to answer those questions, and turning that data into information you can use in decision-making.

In part 2 you developed reports to present your information to the decision makers.

In part 3, we gave you basic information about how to use (and not use) standardized test information and score reports—what is valid and not valid, what is useful and not useful.

Our purpose in this final section is to tie those sections together. We're going to give you some examples of cases where teachers, principals, program managers, superintendents, and boards of trustees use their road maps to answer questions about their goals—and get the information they need to make decisions in their classrooms, schools, and districts.

13

Making Decisions about Individual Students

> Seeking to know is only too often learning to doubt. (Antoinette du ligier de la Garde Deshoulieres, 1638–1694)

We'll start with Mrs. Johnson, a math teacher at Midway Junior High School. Glenn is a student in her seventh-grade homeroom and math class for the 2001–2002 school year. It's the end of the first six weeks. Mrs. Johnson has become increasingly concerned about Glenn's behavior and grades. Although Glenn seems to be bright, he is misbehaving in class, in the halls, and on the bus. He isn't consistently doing his class work and has developed an "oh, well" attitude. As Mrs. Johnson is averaging Glenn's grades, she decides it's time to take a look not only at his current status but also at the pattern of his past performance. Her goal is to positively impact Glenn's behavior and academic achievement. Her question is: What are Glenn's current status and past performance in the areas of academic achievement and discipline?

First she reviews Glenn's discipline referrals for the year. During the first six weeks, he had 9 referrals: 4 for not doing work, 2 for disrespect to a teacher, 2 for bus problems, 1 for running in the hall, and 1 for fighting.

Mrs. Johnson pulls up Glenn's individual student record from his information file. The information is shown in chart 13.1. Take a look at it with her.

Chart 13.1.

Report on Glenn Doherty prepared by Louella Johnson

English Language Arts

		1997-1998	1998-1999	1999-2000	2000-2001
DOHERTY, GLENN DONALD	Proficient	1	1	1	
DOHERTY, GLENN DONALD	Advanced				1

Mathematics

		1997-1998	1998-1999	1999-2000	2000-2001
DOHERTY, GLENN DONALD	Proficient	1	1	1	1

Norm referenced tests

		1997-1998	1999-2000
DOHERTY, GLENN DONALD	SAT9 NCE Total Mathematics	58.51	65.98
DOHERTY, GLENN DONALD	ITBS NCE Math Total	61.62	67.83

School and Teacher grades 3-6

			1997-1998	1998-1999	1999-2000	2000-2001
DOHERTY, GLENN DONALD	Woodbrook Elementary	MILLER, ELIZABETH MONICA	1			
DOHERTY, GLENN DONALD	Woodbrook Elementary	JOHNSON, LINDA CRYSTAL		1		
DOHERTY, GLENN DONALD	Woodbrook Elementary	COFFEY, GONZALO KIM			1	
DOHERTY, GLENN DONALD	Carmel Junior High	SMITH, MARY LAURIE				1
DOHERTY, GLENN DONALD	Carmel Junior High	SHARROW, TODD BARRY				1
DOHERTY, GLENN DONALD	Carmel Junior High	YOUNG, STEVEN RICHARD				1
DOHERTY, GLENN DONALD	Carmel Junior High	NUSSBAUM, RICHARD AUGUSTINE				1
DOHERTY, GLENN DONALD	Carmel Junior High	BASHIR, RITA AMELIA				1
DOHERTY, GLENN DONALD	Carmel Junior High	ARANDA, BARRY PETER				1

Courses

		1997-1998	1998-1999	1999-2000	2000-2001
DOHERTY, GLENN DONALD	Third Grade Homeroom	1			
DOHERTY, GLENN DONALD	Fourth Grade Homeroom		1		
DOHERTY, GLENN DONALD	Fifth Grade Homeroom			1	
DOHERTY, GLENN DONALD	Geography				1
DOHERTY, GLENN DONALD	Civics				1
DOHERTY, GLENN DONALD	English I				1
DOHERTY, GLENN DONALD	Accounting				1
DOHERTY, GLENN DONALD	Geometry				1
DOHERTY, GLENN DONALD	Social Studies				1

Glenn's individual student record contains information from 1997 to 2001, so it goes back to Glenn's third-grade year.

The first thing that Mrs. Johnson notices is that while Glenn scored Proficient in English/language arts on the state CRT in third, fourth, and fifth grades, he scored Advanced, the highest level, in sixth grade. Only 5 percent of the students in the state scored at the Advanced level, so Glenn scored very well on the test.

The next thing she notices is that Glenn scored Proficient in mathematics from third through sixth grades. This means he should have the mathematics background to be successful in seventh grade.

Next she sees the NRT data. He took the SAT9 and the ITBS in third and fifth grades. The report reports NCEs. NCEs don't mean much to Mrs. Johnson, but she knows what national percentile ranks (NPRs) mean, so she refers to table 11.1 to see how the scores equate. In third grade the SAT9 Total Mathematics NCE of 58.51 translates to an NPR at the 66th percentile; the ITBS Math Total NCE of 61.62 translates to an NPR at the 71st percentile. In fifth grade the SAT9 Total Mathematics NCE of 65.98 translates to an NPR at the 77th percentile and the ITBS Math Total NCE of 67.83 translates to an NPR at the 80th percentile. So Mrs. Johnson knows his math achievement is well above average and has improved over time.

A list of schools and teachers appears at the center of Glenn's report. These were Glenn's teachers in the third through sixth grades. Mrs. Johnson plans to call the sixth-grade teachers to ask about Glenn's behavior and work habits last year. Glenn attended Carmel Junior High last year and transferred to Midway Junior High this year. It will be helpful to learn from the Carmel teachers about the differences in the two schools.

The last section on this report gives a list of the courses Glenn has taken. Mrs. Johnson finds the list for sixth grade to be very interesting. In fact, fascinating. Midway doesn't even offer accounting to its sixth graders, and Glenn took it in sixth grade. She needs to ask the accounting teacher at Carmel about that.

Mrs. Johnson's next step is to call Carmel Junior High. She learns that Glenn was a model student at Carmel, was on the principal's honor roll, had perfect attendance, and was a student council representative. He had no discipline referrals. His accounting teacher said that Glenn was a student who was constantly seeking a challenge and had expressed much concern over moving across town to a new school. "Maybe he is having trouble finding friends. Maybe he is not challenged to the level he was here," were comments Mr. Nussbaum made.

Mrs. Johnson thought about that and looked at the data again. She thought that Mr. Nussbaum just might be right. She considered the options. The counselor had a friendship group for new students. She would recommend that Glenn be invited to join it. The school also had a program for high-achieving students; she would recommend Glenn for testing. She'd bet that he'd qualify. The school also had a math academic competition team; she would bring the team members to her class for a mini-competition exhibition and then talk to several students about joining. She was sure Glenn would be one.

Mrs. Johnson smiled to herself. Looking at the data had changed her whole attitude toward Glenn. She'd started with the viewpoint of him as a problem student; now she saw him as a student with whom to build a better relationship to bring out his talents. She was sure her own shift in perspective would make all the difference.

TEACHERS AND PRINCIPALS MAKING DECISIONS ABOUT GROUPS OF STUDENTS

Mr. Jaquiz is the principal of Mohawk Trails Elementary School. Mohawk Trails is known as a good neighborhood school. It has active parent involvement, a satisfied staff, and happy children. Each year fourth-grade students have been tested with a norm-referenced test, but no one has paid much attention to the results. Other grade levels haven't been tested at all. The results have been returned to the school during the summer, and the clerks have put them into the students' cumulative folders.

But this year is different. The state has changed its testing system to a criterion-referenced test based on new state standards. The third, fourth, and fifth grades have been tested. The results have arrived on May 1, with four weeks left in the school year. And, perhaps most important, the data has been disaggregated by ethnicity. This is a first for the district and the school.

Mohawk Trails is a predominately Caucasian (Anglo) school, with small numbers of African American, Asian, and Hispanic students. Since the data have never been disaggregated by ethnicity, Mr. Jaquiz is anxious to see it. He wonders what the reports will show. He knows that sometimes, when data are reported only in the aggregate, differences in performance among groups can be masked by the total. He wonders if this is the case at Mohawk Trails.

Mr. Jaquiz has the score reports on his desk. He is studying the disaggregated data. Charts 13.2a, 13.2b, and 13.2c have the information for you. A separate report is given for mathematics achievement for students in third, fourth, and fifth grades, broken into the student groups of African American, Asian, Caucasian (Anglo), and Hispanic. Achievement is reported in four categories: Below Basic 2, Basic, Proficient, and Advanced. Students who score Below Basic 2 haven't mastered sufficient numbers of objectives to be successful in math. Students who score Basic have mastered enough objectives to be successful, while students who score Proficient have reached mathematics competency, or commended performance, on the state test.

Looking at the third-grade report, Mr. Jaquiz first sees that small numbers of African American, Asian, and Hispanic students took the test (a total of 13). He knows that when the numbers are small, he needs to be very careful drawing conclusions about the groups of students and needs to look at the individuals' performances instead. He needs to also be careful when discussing the performance not to use information that would allow people to know who these children are, since the numbers are small enough that they might be identifiable. There are some conclusions he can draw, however. They are listed here:

- No African American or Hispanic students scored in the Proficient category.

Chart 13.2a.

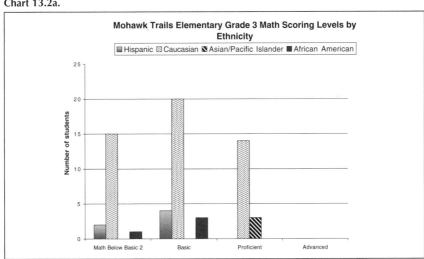

Chart 13.2b.

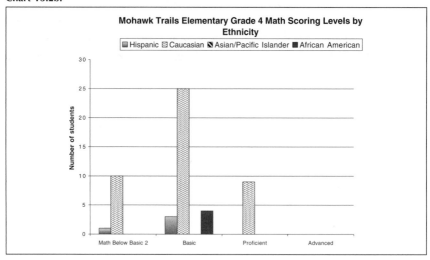

Chart 13.2c.

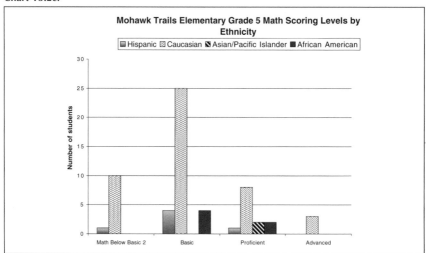

- The Caucasian students' performance falls roughly into a bell-shaped curve, with 15 students in Below Basic 2, 20 in Basic, and 14 in Proficient.
- Of the Asian students, 3 scored in Proficient.
- No third-graders scored Advanced.

Looking at the fourth-grade report, Mr. Jaquiz noticed, that, once again, there were small numbers of African American, Hispanic, and Asian students, a total of 13. Seventy-five Caucasian students took the test. He'll have to be careful drawing conclusions and reporting information from the fourth-grade report, too, when considering the 13 students. In addition, he noticed the following:

- No African American, Hispanic, or Asian students scored Proficient.
- The scores of all students clustered in the Basic category, with a total of 32 of the 52 students in the Basic group.
- No students scored Advanced.

Looking at the fifth-grade scores, Mr. Jaquiz counted 14 students who were African American, Asian, or Hispanic, and 46 Caucasian students. Once again, he will have to be careful how he reports the data and with the conclusions he draws. He noticed the following about the data:

- No African American, Asian, or Hispanic students scored at the Advanced level.
- Three Caucasian students scored at the Advanced level.
- The performance of the Caucasian students for the other three levels was very much like a normal distribution, with 10 in Below Basic 2, 25 in Basic, and 8 in Proficient.

Mr. Jaquiz immediately knew that the school needed to develop a plan for increasing student achievement and that this plan should include strategies for closing the gaps among the student groups.

Because the school had never seen disaggregated data, they had not set a goal for closing the achievement gaps among student groups. So Mr. Jaquiz set a goal: Close the gaps in mathematics achievement among the student groups at Mohawk Trails Elementary School by raising the achievement of the lower-achieving student groups. The question has been answered: Is there a gap in achievement among achievement in identified groups in this school for the following groups: African American, Caucasian, Asian, and Hispanic. The answer is yes.

Mr. Jaquiz knows that it will take a team planning and implementation effort to deal with the gaps and to close them. He decides that his first step is to set a meeting of the campus leadership team to review the data in detail and begin an in-depth analysis of what it means. At the meeting, the team decides to do the following:

- Examine how well the teachers prepared the students to take the test.
- Consider the match between the curriculum they taught and the curriculum that was tested on the state test.
- Set up a complete analysis of the test data, including an item analysis and an analysis of objectives mastered by students to search for patterns.
- Analyze differences in performance among classes and groups within classes.
- Interview parents of students who didn't master the standards to learn their perspective as to why their children didn't do well on the test.
- Set up a plan for students who did not master the standards on the test.
- Search for patterns in the data to make predictions that will enable them to be proactive in the future.

Mr. Jaquiz thinks they have a good starting point for their first year using a CRT and disaggregated data, but he knows they have their work cut out for them in closing the gap.

PROGRAM MANAGERS MAKING DECISIONS ABOUT PROGRAMS

When program managers weigh the value of a program, generally they compare the benefits to students with the cost of the program, seeking programs that give the biggest benefit for the cost. That sounds simple, but in fact, can be quite complex. It is made more difficult by the fact that in a school, students are rarely simply placed in one program for treatment, like they would be in an experimental setting. So it is hard to say with absolute certainty that this program or that program was the defining reason for a student's success or failure. That is another place where we look at trends and patterns to make our judgment calls.

Mrs. Blackcloud is the reading coordinator for Southpoint School District. She has been instrumental in piloting three different reading programs for the school district and has been monitoring and studying the pilot programs for the last three years. The latest achievement data has just come in and she is studying it now. Her program goal is to improve reading achievement for the students in the district. Her questions are: Do programs A, B, or C improve reading achievement? Are programs A, B, or C cost-effective? The data are shown in chart 13.3.

Chart 13.3.

		Average per Student Cost	Grade 2	Grade 3	Change Grade 2 to Grade 3	Grade 4	Change Grade 3 to Grade 4	Grade 5	Change Grade 4 to Grade 5
Mean ELA Scaled Score	Program A	$350	300.14	402.87	102.73	507.08	104.19	610.23	103.17
Mean ELA Scaled Score	Program B	$30	302.78	435.63	132.85	507.16	71.53	611.17	104.01
Mean ELA Scaled Score	Program C	$125	299.34	502.81	203.47	510.44	7.63	544.1	33.66

The reading programs are listed as program A, B, and C. Each program was piloted in one school. The students started the pilot program in second grade, then continued in third, fourth, and fifth grades. This data is for the first group of students to complete the pilot program through fifth grade. When making program decisions, it's important to look at programs over time, and not make snap judgments. That's why the district has been piloting three different programs in three schools and keeping data on each for three years. That way they can see trends and patterns and make a better decision than simply choosing one program off the shelf and putting it into all the schools immediately.

The average cost per pupil is given for each program. Program A cost $350 per student. Program B cost $30 per student. Program C cost $125 per student.

Scores are given as mean scaled scores for each school. A year's growth is 100 points. So if a student scored 300 in second grade, 400 in third grade, 500 in fourth grade, and 600 in fifth grade, he would have made one year's growth each year. If a student scored 300 in second grade and 415 in third grade, he made more than a year's growth. Likewise, if a student scored 300 in second grade and 385 in fourth grade, he made less than a year's growth.

Mrs. Blackcloud looked at the data for reading program A. The mean scaled score change remained relatively constant from second to fifth grade, with the change each time over 100—102.73, 104.19, and 103.17. The mean scaled score by fifth grade was 610.23, above the average mean scaled score of 600.

Looking at the data for program B, Mrs. Blackcloud saw that it was much more variable. The mean scaled score by fifth grade was at 611.17, about the same as program A. But the change score didn't grow in equal increments. The change score was big from second grade to third grade (132.85), then was much smaller from third to fourth grade (71.53), and back up again from fourth to fifth (104.01).

Looking at the data for program C, Mrs. Blackcloud saw that that was the only one of the three programs that had a mean scaled score less than the full three years' growth. The fifth-grade mean scaled score was only 544.1, far below the 600 mean scaled score she was expecting as a minimum. She had been concerned last year when the data had shown a small gain (7.63), but the gain the first year had been so big (203.47) that she and the principal had decided to try the program one more year. At this point, with only a 33.66 gain and a mean scaled score of 544.1, she knew it was time to abandon program C.

But what about programs A and B? The results at fifth grade were nearly the same. But the cost was certainly different. In this time of huge budget cuts, she knew that program B would be much more sustainable over the long haul for the district and could be ramped up to scale in all the schools. Her recommendation to the superintendent would be to go forward with program B as the district's reading program, based on the results of the study and the cost-effectiveness of the program. She'd express a word of caution, however, that they'd need to watch the implementation because of the variability in the second year's gains.

SUPERINTENDENTS AND BOARDS OF TRUSTEES
MAKING DECISIONS ABOUT DISTRICTS

Dr. Wholpol was the new superintendent in Westminster School District, a 13,000-student district. It was October, and he had just arrived in the district. He knew that plans were in place for improvements in student achievement. He had studied the district improvement plan and knew that student achievement had been steadily improving over the last few years. He did want to look at some of the achievement data himself. The district's goal was to improve student achievement in the areas of math and English language arts. His questions were: What was the level of achievement on the most recent state tests? Was there any correlation between the achievement on the math and the English language arts achievement in the district?

He got charts with the achievement on the state CRT in math and English language arts for the aggregate scores of the district's third- through eighth-graders, a total of about 6,000 students. He began to study them. The information is shown on charts 13.4a and 13.4b.

The English language arts test scores are divided into five categories, Below Basic 1, Below Basic 2, Basic, Proficient, and Advanced. Students who perform Below Basic 1 and 2 are not successful in English. Students who perform in the Proficient and Advanced categories are very successful. Chart 13.4a shows the count of students in each category for Westminster School District.

Chart 13.4a.

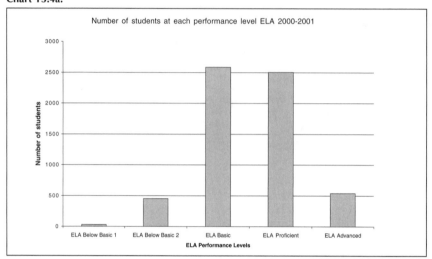

The mathematics test scores are divided into the same five categories. Chart 13.4b shows the count of students in each category for Westminster School District.

When Mr. Wholpol studied the two charts, he noticed that many more students scored Proficient in English language arts than scored Proficient in math. He knew the data were for the same students and began to won-

Chart 13.4b.

	2000–2001
ELA Below Basic 1	29
ELA Below Basic 2	452
ELA Basic	2,585
ELA Proficient	2,504
ELA Advanced	540

Chart 13.4c.

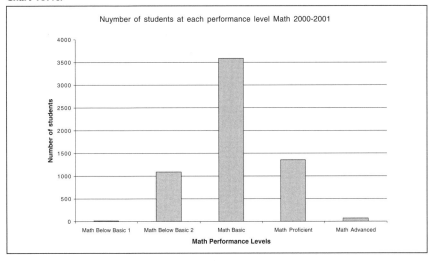

Chart 13.4d.

	2000–2001
Math Below Basic 1	14
Math Below Basic 2	1,089
Math Basic	3,587
Math Proficient	1,353
Math Advanced	67

der about the relationship between the two tests, so he ran another chart (chart 13.5). This chart compares the English language arts test scores with the math test scores.

When he studied charts like this, Mr. Wholpol had come to expect that the data would generally fall in a diagonal line. Students would usually score in the same category in both subject areas, with a few exceptions. So he would have predicted that the biggest group of scores would go through the matched boxes—for example, English language arts Advanced and math Advanced. The intersection of those two categories is a matched box, as is the intersection of each of the other sets of categories, Proficient, Basic, and Below Basic 1 and 2.

His prediction was true for Below Basic 2, where 442 students scored Below Basic 2 in both math and English language arts, and Basic, where

Chart 13.5.

	2000–2001 ELA Below Basic 1	2000–2001 ELA Below Basic 2	2000–2001 ELA Basic	2000–2001 ELA Proficient	2000–2001 ELA Advanced
Math Below Basic 1	4	10			
Math Below Basic 2		442	647		
Math Basic			1,938	1,649	
Math Proficient				855	498
Math Advanced	25				42

1,938 students scored Basic. However, it wasn't true for the other three categories. Mr. Wholpol found that interesting and decided to see what it meant, if he could.

A large number of students scored one category lower in math than they did in English language arts. This was true for English language arts Advanced, where 498 math students scored Proficient, with only 42 scoring Advanced. It was true for English language arts Proficient, where 1,649 students scored math Basic, with 855 scoring Proficient. Mr. Wholpol noticed this and decided to look at the difficulty of the math test versus the English language arts test—was it simply a more difficult test? Or were there other reasons that students were scoring lower?

In addition, while looking at the chart, Mr. Wholpol saw that four students scored Below Basic 1 in both math and English language arts. That made sense to him, and he decided to find out who those students were and see what special help they were receiving, since they were not succeeding in either subject area.

Surprisingly, he noticed that 25 students scored Advanced on the math test and Below Basic 1 on the English language arts test. He wondered how it could be that a student could score in the top 5 percent of all the students in the state in math, and in the bottom 10 percent in English language arts. That was a puzzle. He decided to follow up on those students. He really wanted to understand how that could happen.

At this point, Mr. Wholpol had a number of avenues to explore. He was glad he had asked the questions.

14

The Journey Ends . . . or Does It?

> Learning . . . should be a job and full of excitement. It is life's
> greatest adventure; it is an illustrated excursion into the minds
> of noble and learned men, not a conducted tour through a jail.
> (Taylor Caldwell, 1900–1985)

You picked up this book because you wanted to develop a road map to
make information-based decisions. Now you are at the last chapter of the
book, but does that mean you are at the end of the road? You may wish
that were so, but to quote our old friend Yogi Berra one more time, "When
you come to a fork in the road, take it."

You're not at the end of the road, you're at one fork in the road. The
road goes on and on. And it will fork again and again. The journey of using information to make decisions doesn't have an end. We expect you
knew that when you started. It's like most things in life that are worth a
major investment of time, resources, and commitment. Why would you
invest so much in this process if you were just going to make a decision
or two and then put everything on the shelf, sit down, and drink coffee?

The good news is that you and your team have done the hard part of the
work. You have gotten everything together and you have it in one place.
Congratulations!!

We think you deserve a celebration worthy of the Fourth of July or New Year's Eve! This is a big accomplishment.

As we wave good-bye to you on your journey, we do want to give you a few going-away presents, pointers that will help you on your road. For those of you who read the last chapter first, these will be new. For those who've read the whole book, you've heard them before.

> **If we value the pursuit of knowledge, we must be free to follow wherever that search may lead us. (Adlai E. Stevenson Jr.)**

- *Use your goals as the basis for the questions you ask.* We've said this more than once, but it is an important point. Otherwise you can collect lots of data, analyze it to death, and still have nothing that helps you in decision-making. Start with your goals first. You can't go wrong if your goals are your starting place.

- *Use the questions you need to answer as the basis for the data you collect.* Collect data based on your questions. Stifle the urge to collect those "interesting-but-unnecessary" items. Knowing your questions tells you the data that will be important to collect. You can collect a lot of data, and spend a lot of time and energy collecting them, but never use them. The purpose of data collection is to be able to answer those important questions. So use the questions as the basis for collecting data.

- *Maintain an open-ended system.* This will allow you to ask other questions and input additional data. Just when you think you've asked all the questions you could possibly want to answer, you'll think of the most important question ever. Or the state legislature or federal government will pass a law that will require you to provide information in a new and unheard-of way. Having an open-ended, flexible system will enable you to modify your inputs so that you can obtain the outputs you need over time. Nothing is more frustrating than to have the system just the way you want it, and then have it become obsolete.

- *Have a structure for your work.* Pay attention to the system as a whole and develop each component of the system so that the parts work seamlessly together. This handbook is all about giving structure to your work and developing a system. The value to having a system is that it can be developed, maintained, and replicated.

- *Pay attention to the processes.* Processes must be detailed, written down, and followed. That's why we recommend a data notebook and master data directory, along with your information-based decision-making road map. Together these tools form your master plan. Capturing your processes enables you to monitor and improve them.

- *Data analysis helps you answer questions—it doesn't answer questions for you.* Data analysis gives you information. Information is the basis for your decision-making. You will answer the question yourself. Always look beyond and behind the information to see what is really there. Avoid making decisions based on surface-level information.

• *Double-check your use of test terminology and measurements* before
  you make decisions using standardized test data, using the information found in part 3 of this handbook, Test Primer.

The data-collection process can sometimes pinpoint places and ways
to make your school system more efficient in a broader sense than
data collection itself. In some ways, processes serve to define the
system, since processes are where the leadership of the system
works to obtain the results the system wants to obtain. The better the
processes, the more efficient and effective the system and the more
likely it will obtain the results it wishes to obtain.

Dr. Delaney, the superintendent of Mt. Carmel School District,
was committed to using data to make decisions. She read the handbook *Refining Common Sense* and decided that it gave her a way to
develop a road map for getting her district's data together to be able
to use its data to make decisions. She gathered her leadership team
together, and they began to follow the process in the guidebook to
collect their data. Within three weeks she had learned the following
things:

• The free/reduced lunch information had more than 20 percent
  of the students listed as "unknown."
• Information on students who had been retained was only available in individual student cumulative folders; there was no
  master list.
• Three different people kept a file with the same SAT data, using it for the same purpose.
• No one knew where the records were for teachers who had attended professional development.

Dr. Delaney began to make a list of questions for her team to consider making the team more efficient, relating not only to data collection, but to operations as a whole:

- Which of these situations indicates a system failure or major system problem?
- How will we resolve the system problems?
- How can we make this part of our system more efficient?
- How can we simplify this part of our system?
- How can we eliminate redundancies in this part of our system?

What questions would you add to her list? What questions would you ask about your system? Which of those questions are limited to the data-collection process? Which are questions about the bigger system?

Our final point is to remember that the reason you are doing this—expending all this time and energy—is to improve your school and district for the children who go to school there. And the children who are in school now are worth your best effort. This year's first-graders won't have another chance to be in first grade. The children who are in school next Tuesday won't have another chance to learn what they are supposed to that day. When your seniors walk across the stage, they go out into the world with the preparation you have given them. For every one of the children, every day matters. And every decision you make matters. So the more information you have, the better those decisions can be, the more each child benefits. And we all know that makes every minute you spend working in your school a worthwhile investment of your time.

Bibliography

Adam, E., & Quinn, J. (2002, January). Using data to get results. *Education Update, 44*(1). www.ascd.org/publications/edupdate/200201/12.html [accessed March 28, 2003].

Adams, F. P. *The quotations page.* www.quotationspage.com.

American Association of School Administrators. (2002). *Using data to improve schools: What's working.* Arlington, VA: Author.

American Association of School Administrators. (2003). *Successful strategies for district data reporting in the era of No Child Left Behind.* Arlington, VA: Author.

American Productivity & Quality Center. (2002). *Erase the gap: Achieving excellence through ADAPTS.* Houston, TX: Education Initiative.

Ardovino, J., Hollingsworth, J., & Ybarra, S. (2000). *Multiple measures: Accurate ways to assess student achievement.* Thousand Oaks, CA: Corwin Press.

Baker, S. (2002). *The complete idiot's guide to business statistics.* Indianapolis, IN: Alpha Books.

Barnes, F. V., & Miller, M. (2001, April). Data analysis by walking around. *The School Administrator, 58*(4), 20–25.

Barron, P., Behrends, C., & Feeney, J. Learning to use data to get results. *EncOnline.* www.enc.org [accessed March 25, 2003].

Bernhardt, V. L. (1998). *Data analysis for comprehensive schoolwide improvement.* Larchmont, NY: Eye on Education.

Bernhardt, V. L. (2000a). *Designing and using databases for school improvement.* Larchmont, NY: Eye on Education.

Bernhardt, V. L. (2000b). *The example school portfolio.* Larchmont, NY: Eye on Education.

Bernhardt, V. L. (2000c, Winter). Intersections: New routes open when one type of data crosses another. *Journal of Staff Development 21*(1). www.nsdc.org/library/jsd/bernhardt211.html [accessed March 25, 2003].

Bernhardt, V. L. (2002). *The school portfolio toolkit: A planning, implementation, and evaluation guide for continuous school improvement.* Larchmont, NY: Eye on Education.

Berra, Y. (1998). *I really didn't say everything I said.* New York: Workman.

Bost, E. M., & Newman, S. B. (2002, December 17). Joint education/agriculture letter about the use of student information collected pursuant to the national school lunch program. www.ed.gov/offices/OESE/SASA/letter121702.html [accessed June 21, 2003].

Bracey, G. W. (1997). *Understanding education statistics: It's easier (and more important) than you think.* Arlington, VA: Educational Research Service.

Bracey, G. W. (2000). *Bail me out!* Thousand Oaks, CA: Corwin Press.

Brittain, D. (2003, May). My database will call your database, but can they talk? A primer on data reporting compatibility. *T.H.E. Journal, 30*(10), 12–14.

Brown, J. L., & Moffett, C.A. (1999). *The hero's journey: How educators can transform schools and improve learning.* Alexandria, VA: Association for Supervision and Curriculum Development.

Caldwell, T. www.creativequotations.com/one/2001.htm.

Canada, B. O. (2001, April). Welcome more data, but apply it well. *The School Administrator, 58*(4), 44.

Carroll, S. R., and Carroll, D. J. (2002). *Statistics made simple for school leaders.* Lanham, MD: Scarecrow Press.

Checklist for interpreting student achievement data: Cautions for testing interpretations. (1999, August). *The Master Teacher's VIP Administrative Solutions, 31*(1), 1–2.

Cleveland, W. S. (1985). *The elements of graphing data.* Monterey, CA: Wadsworth Advanced Books and Software.

Cleveland, W. S. (1993). *Visualizing data.* Murray Hill, NJ: ATT&T Laboratories.

Cohen, F. (2003, May). Mining data to improve teaching. *Educational Leadership, 60*(8), 53–56.

Collins, J. (2001). *Good to great: Why some companies make the leap . . . and others don't.* New York: Harper Business.

Conzemius, A., & O'Neill, J. (2002). *The handbook for SMART school teams.* Bloomington, IN: National Educational Service.

Creighton, T. B. (2001a, April). Data analysis in administrators' hands: An oxymoron? *The School Administrator, 58*(4), 6–11.

Creighton, T. B. (2001b). *Schools and data: The educator's guide for using data to improve decision making.* Thousand Oaks, CA: Corwin Press.

Curtis, D. (2002, January 21). Learning by the numbers. *Edutopia.* glef.org/ FMPro?-DB=articles1.fp5&-format=article.html [accessed March 25, 2003].

Data-driven decision making. (2000, Summer). *School Governance & Leadership, 3*(2), 6–7, 12.

Deck, S. (2000, November 1). This goes on your permanent record. *Data Warehousing.* www.cio.com/archive/110100/permanent_content.html [accessed March 25, 2002].

de la Garde Deshoulieres, A. www.fool.com/news/take/2003/take030407.

Doyle, D. P. (2003, May). Data-driven Decision-making: Is it the mantra of the month or does it have staying power? *T.H.E. Journal, 30*(10), 19–21.

Doyle, D. P., & Pimentel, S. (1999). *Raising the standard: An eight-step action guide for schools and communities* (2nd ed.). Thousand Oaks, CA: Corwin Press.

Delehant, A. (2000, December). *Creating change by using data.* Paper presented at the National Staff Development Council annual conference, December 4, 2000, Atlanta, GA.

Disraeli, B. *The quotations page.* www.quotationspage.com/quotes/Benjamin _Disraeli.

Gay, L. R., & Airasian, P. (2000). *Educational research: Competencies for analysis and application* (6th ed.). Upper Saddle River, NJ: Prentice-Hall.

Gemberling, K. W., Smith, C. W., & Villani, J. S. (2000). *The key work of school boards guidebook.* Alexandria, VA: National School Boards Association.

Goens, G. A. (2001, April). Beyond data: The world of scenario planning. *The School Administrator, 58*(4), 27–30, 32.

Goldman, J. P. (2001, April). Dealing with the data dump. *The School Administrator, 58*(4), 5.

Holcomb, E. L. (1999). *Getting excited about data: How to combine people, passion, and proof.* New York: Corwin Press.

Houston, P. D. (2000, Summer). School boards and technology. *School Governance & Leadership, 3*(2), 15.

Keeney, L. (1998, May). *Using data for school improvement.* Providence, RI: Annenberg Institute for School Reform at Brown University.

Killion, J., & Bellamy, G. T. (2000, Winter). On the job: Data analysts focus school improvement efforts. *Journal of Staff Development, 21*(1). www.nsdc. org/library/jsd/killion211.html [accessed March 25, 2003].

Kongshem, L. (1999, September). *Mining the school district data warehouse.* Electronic School, 14–17.

Kosslyn, S. M. (1994). *Elements of graph design.* New York: W. H. Freeman and Company.

Levesque, K., Bradby, D., Rossi, K., and Teitelbaum, P. (1998). *At your fingertips: Using everyday data to improve schools.* Berkeley, CA: MPR Associates.

Liddle, K. (2000, March). *Data-driven success.* www.electronic-school.com [accessed March 25, 2003].

Love, N. (2001). *Using data/getting results: A practical guide to school improvement in mathematics and science.* Norwood, MA: Christopher Gordon.

Milne, A. A. (1926). *Winnie-the-Pooh.* New York: E. P. Dutton.

Nichols, B. W., & Singer, K. P. (2000, February). Developing data mentors. *Educational Leadership, 57*(5), 34–37.

Noyce, P., Perda, D., & Traver, R. (2000, February). Creating data-driven schools. *Educational Leadership, 57*(5), 52–56.

O'Neill, J. (2000, February). SMART goals, SMART schools. *Educational Leadership, 57*(5), 46–50.

Payer, A. (2000) *Introduction to formalien of scientific work.* www.payer.de/wissarbeit/wissarb01.htm [accessed June 21, 2003].

Peters, T. (1987). *Thriving on chaos.* New York: Alfred A. Knopf.

Plunkett, S. (2002, September 29). Sermon. St. Andrew Presbyterian Church, Denton, TX. www.saint-andrew.com/pdfs/0929_02sermon.pdf [accessed June 21, 2003].

Popham, W. J. (1999). *Classroom assessment: What teachers need to know.* (2nd ed.). Boston: Allyn & Bacon.

Popham, W. J. (2000) *Testing! testing! What every parent should know about school tests.* Boston: Allyn & Bacon.

Protheroe, N. (2001, Summer). Improving teaching and learning with data-based decisions: Asking the right questions and acting on the answers. *ERS Spectrum.* www.ers.org/spectrum/sum01a/html [accessed March 24, 2003].

Rand, P. (1993). *Design, form and chaos.* New Haven, CT: Yale University Press.

Ready, D. E. (2001, Spring). Collaborative inquiry uses data to get results. *Hands On, 24*(1).

Richardson, J. (2000, October/November). *The numbers game: Measure progress by analyzing data.* NSDC Tools for Schools.

Sandifer, P. (1999, June). *Project report: The development of a management information system for Laurens County School District 56.* Clinton, SC.

Savary, L. M. (1992). *Creating quality schools.* Arlington, VA: American Association of School Administrators.

Schlechty, P. C. (1997). *Inventing better schools.* San Francisco, CA: Jossey-Bass.

Schlechty, P. C. (2002): *Working on the work: An action plan for teachers, principals, and superintendents.* San Francisco, CA: Jossey-Bass.

Schmoker, M. (1996). *Results: The key to continuous school improvement.* Alexandria, VA: Association for Supervision and Curriculum Development.

Schmoker, M. (1999). *Results: The key to continuous school improvement* (2nd ed.). Alexandria, VA: Association for Supervision and Curriculum Development.

Schmoker, M. (2000, October). *Results-driven professional development*. Paper presented at Fall 2000 Conference of South Carolina Staff Development Council and South Carolina Department of Education, Charleston, SC.

Schmoker, M. (2001). *The results fieldbook: Practical strategies from dramatically improved schools*. Alexandria, VA: Association for Supervision and Curriculum Development.

Schmoker, M., & Wilson, R. B. (1993). *Total quality education: Profiles of schools that demonstrate the power of Deming's management principles*. Bloomington, IN: Phi Delta Kappa.

Senge, P. (1990). *The fifth discipline: The art and practice of the learning organization*. New York: Doubleday.

Stevenson, A., Jr. (1952). *The quotations page*. www.quotationspage.com.

Streifer, P. A. (2001, April). The "drill down" process. *The School Administrator, 58*(4), 6–11.

Streifer, P. A. (2002). *Using data to make better educational decisions*. Lanham, MD: Scarecrow Press.

Tufte, E. R. (1983). *The visual display of quantitative information*. Cheshire, CT: Graphics Press.

Tufte, E. R. (1997). *Visual explanations: Images and quantities, evidences and narrative*. Cheshire, CT: Graphics Press.

U.S. Department of Education, National Center for Education Statistics, & National Forum on Education Statistics. (2000, October). *Building an automated student record system: A step-by-step guide for local and state education agencies*. Washington, DC: Author.

von Szent-Gyorgyi, Albert. *The quotations page*. www.quotationspage.com.

Wade, H. H. (2001, December). Data inquiry and analysis for educational reform. *ERIC Digest 153*. eric.uoregon.edu/publications/digests/digest153.html [accessed March 25, 2003].

Wolf, D. P., & White, A. M. (2000, February). Charting the course of student growth. *Educational Leadership, 57*(5), 6–11.

Yeagley, R. (2001, April). Data in your hands. *The School Administrator, 58*(4), 12–15.

Zigrossi, S. (2001, September). *Connecting data with accountability: The Texas story*. Paper presented at the Texas Association of School Administrators/Texas Association of School Boards annual convention for the Charles A. Dana Center at the University of Texas at Austin.

Index

About the Authors

Vickie Williams Phelps, Ed.D., is superintendent of the Taylor Independent School District in Taylor, Texas. She is a 29-year educator who has been superintendent in three districts in two states.

Elizabeth F. Warren, J.D., Ph.D., has more than 20 years of experience in public education, having served as an assistant superintendent, consortium director, and government relations legal counsel. She is president and CEO of Educational Policy Initiatives Corp., an educatioal consulting firm.